AF305219

ISSUE NUMBER ONE
THE
THE
REMOVAL
TECHNICIAN

Proud to be an Embalmer

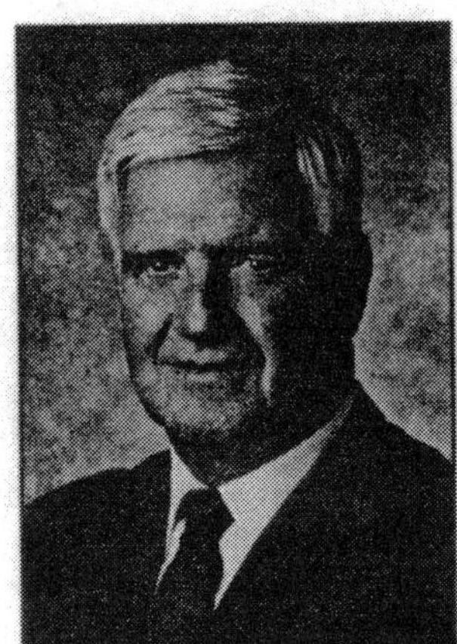

Maurice E. Newnam III

As I sat down to write this article, I could not help but think about the time I spent in mortuary college embalming classes and labs as I struggled to learn the skill of embalming. I remembered the time spent trying to raise a popliteal artery, an artery that I had never heard of at home, or the time spent trying to duplicate a nose out of wax, a skill that came easily to some in my class but not to me.

I have since realized this time was spent learning the most important of skills—one that could help a family immeasurably as they go through the process of grief. The importance of the memory picture created by the properly embalmed and restored loved one is something that we must never lose sight of and never be ashamed to ask permission to do. We must take the time to accomplish this even though we may have already been at work for many hours. We must provide the funds to have the most modern, up-to-date embalming facilities, equipment and chemicals available.

As an art and science, embalming is the one time that we can really help families by using the skills and techniques that we have learned and honed over a long period of time. Embalming is a skill that is uniquely ours, and one that is not provided by the memorial societies, the casket stores and others that claim to be "death care" providers.

Though, the people in our communities see us as many different things—civic leaders, small business owners, funeral directors, caregivers, counselors, parents and neighbors—we are seldom thought of as the embalmer. Be proud of the fact that you have this skill and that you know the importance of your work to families that have just suffered a loss.

With the acceptance of our role as the embalmer, we also accept the challenge of keeping up to date on modern techniques and chemicals that are being made available. We accept the challenge of knowing and abiding by the myriad of regulations from the Environmental Protection Agency and the Occupational Safety and Health Administration that are put in place to protect the health and well-being of ourselves, our employees and the public. We accept the importance of attending continuing education courses and seminars offered by our state associations and NFDA so that we may continue to quietly offer the best in funeral service care of which embalming is an integral part.

Hold your head high, take care in the work you do and be proud to be an embalmer.

Maurice E. Newnam III

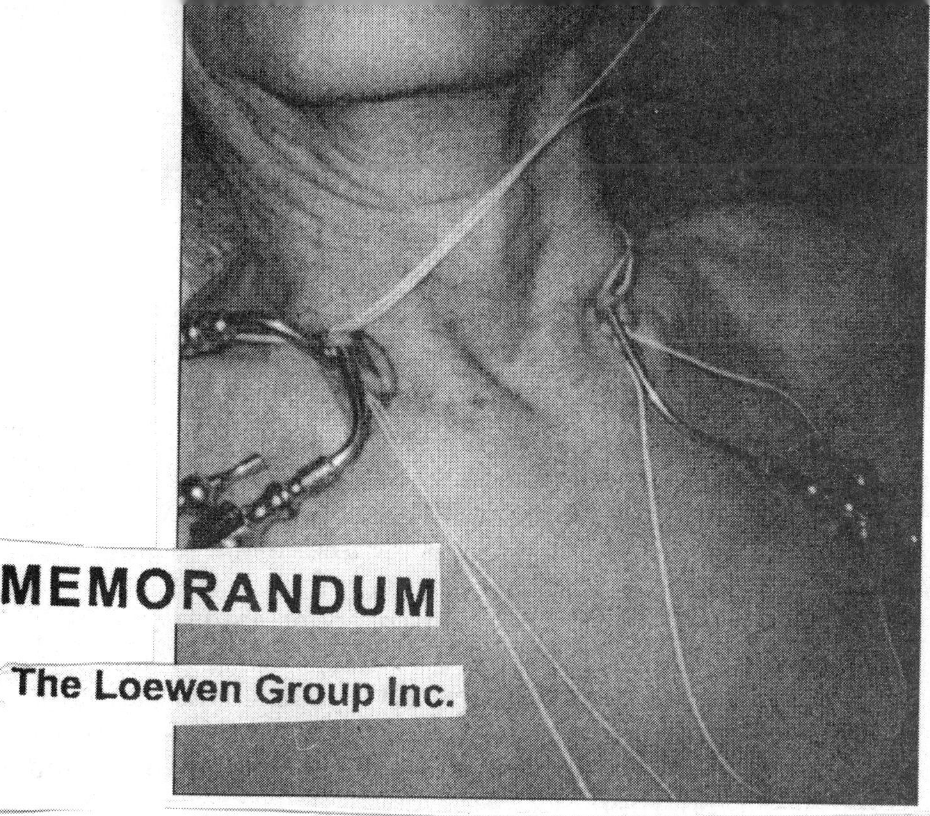

MEMORANDUM

The Loewen Group Inc.

TO: All Loewen Locations
c.c. Presidents, Regional Partners, Regional Managers

FROM: Dave Laundy, Vice-President, Corporate Communications

DATE: May 16, 1997

RE: Media Attention

We are all justifiably proud of our Company, its values and successes, and of the quality service we provide. But we must also be aware that there are those whose agenda is not to depict either our Company or funeral and cemetery service in a positive light.

Media attention to our industry has increased of late and there is always the possibility that anyone in our Company could be contacted directly by media people with little or no advance notice. This could take the form of a telephone call or the unannounced arrival of a camera crew. It is important that you not allow yourself to be caught off guard.

Loewen's policy is to be as co-operative with the media as possible, particularly those we know. But this process must be managed carefully.

Should a media representative call you or arrive at your door, be polite but do not volunteer any information or answer any questions. Explain that you must first contact the Company's Communications Department. Then call me directly, at one of the following numbers:

Office 604-293-7857
Home 604-980-1208
Cel 604-817-5566

Should you find yourself in this situation, be assured we will work with you and your regional manager to determine the appropriate course of action.

It's important to have an accurate picture of the type of people working for the Loewen Comany.

Dan & Alex- We write most of this publication.

Ernie Gatchell- Ernie is about fifty seven years old and he's the head funeral director at Gables. He gave us the T.V. and microwave that we have in our office. Ernie's picture is on the back cover.

Bill Briscoe- Bill is the manager of the Portland Service Center (We work for the Portland Service Center and our office is located in Gable and Parkrose Funeral Home). He is probably in his early forties and he has two children. Bill has only been in the funeral industry for around six years.

Glenn Dixon- Glenn is also in his early forties and he has at least one child. Glenn seems to be second in command to Bill in the management of the Portland Service Center. Glenn moved here from Southern California and he's like annis liquour and bourbon.

Barry Dillinger- Barry Dillinger is twenty five, has blonde hair, is married, and has one child. After five years in the army Barry obtained an apprenticeship at a funeral home in Lebanon (south of Salem) He moved to Portland in order to work for Peg Paxson funeral home in Beaverton and attend school.

Sandra Wright- Sandra is twenty nine, has two children, lives in Gresham, and has been married three times (she's currently divorced, but is dating a man named Ken who works for another removal service). Sandra is probably the most attractive woman working in the funeral industry.

Joe Snell- Joe Snell is twenty seven and lives in Oregon City with his parents. Joe is about forty pounds overweight, wears black boots, and has given up a career as a firefighter. He's now pursuing a job with the Oregon Department of Corrections.

Erin Fortin- Erin is also in his late twenties, and moved to Portland after graduating from a university in Montana with a degree in psychology. Erin was a grunt in the marines for six years and has huge shoulders and no neck.

Jason Pfau- Jason is in a band called the Deliquents. His band recently received five thousand dollars for recording a punk version of the theme from the Wide World of Sports. Jason has demonic tattoos on his wrists and a stud in his tongue.

the Modern
Preparation Room

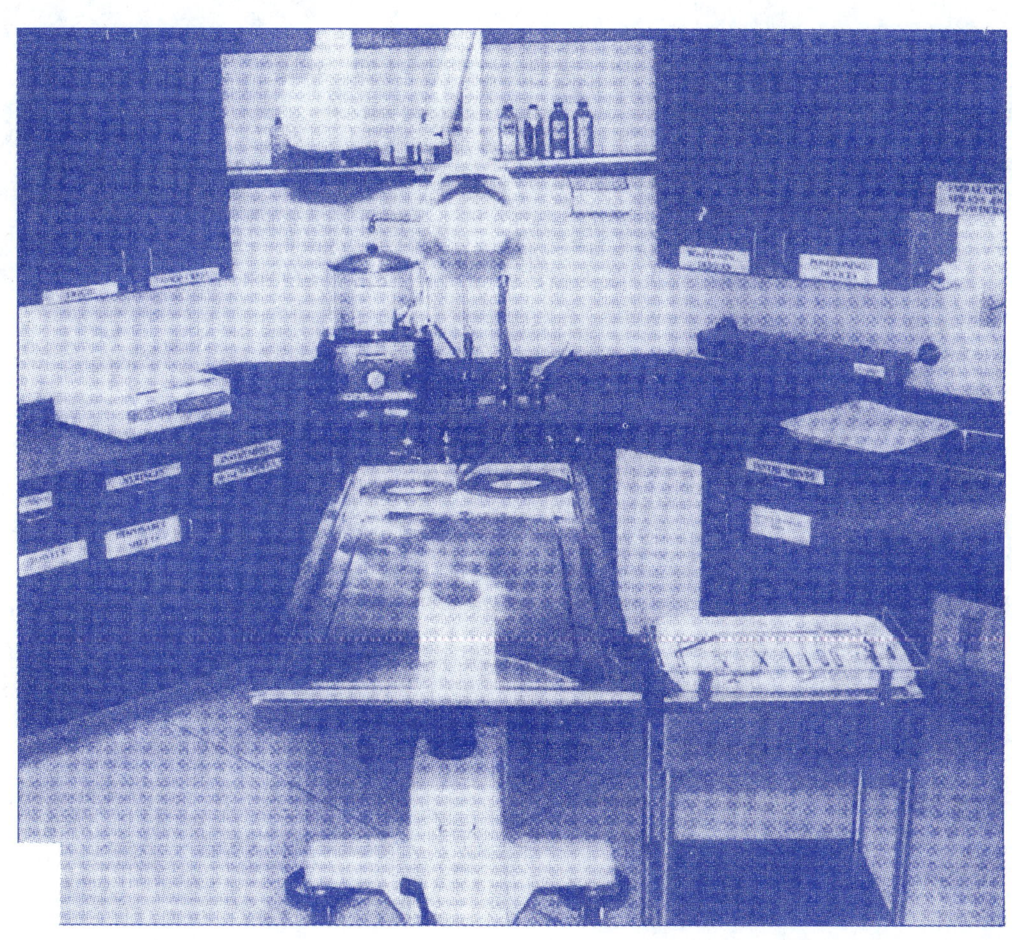

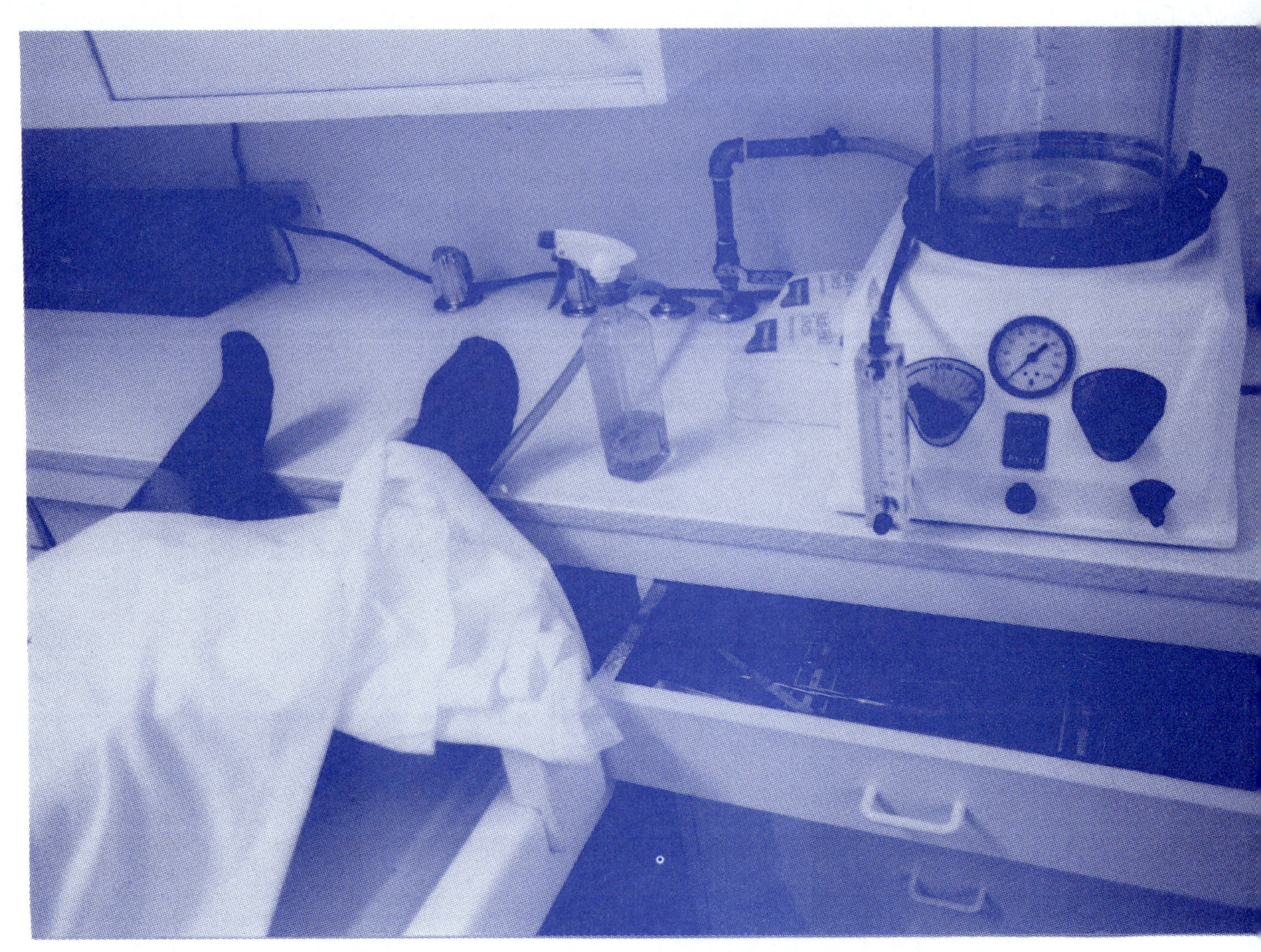

In this case, the table water supply is green, the embalming machine water supply is yellow and the aspirator water supply is red.

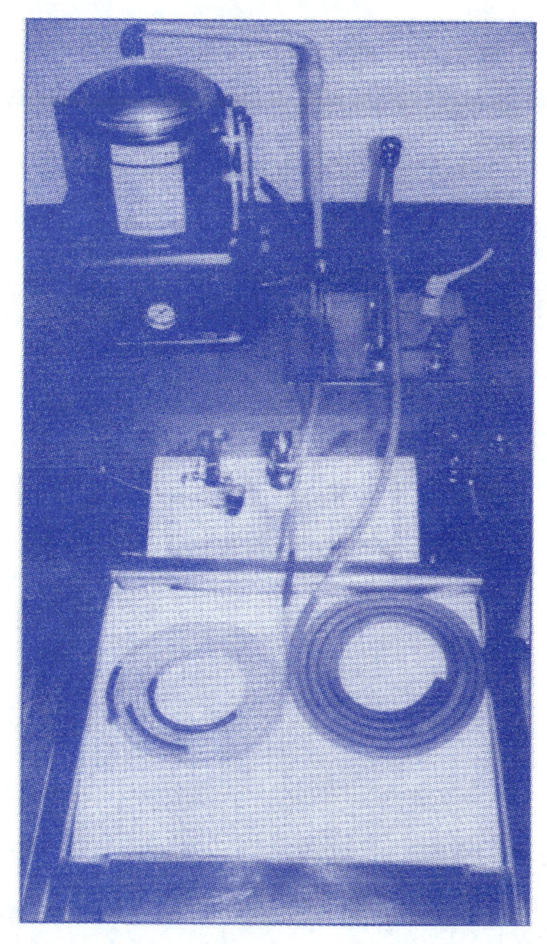

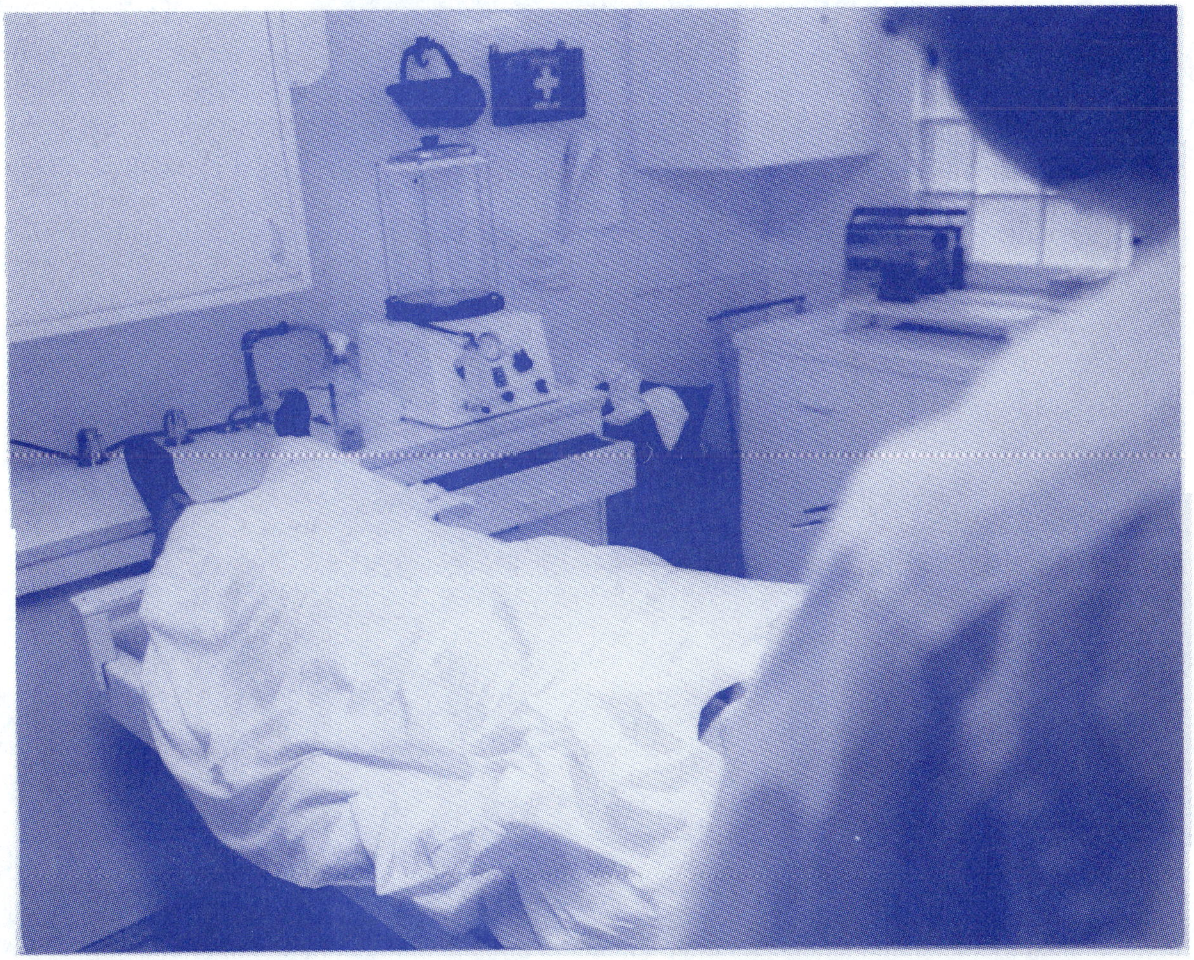

This system is especially beneficial in preparation rooms used by many embalmers, those who embalm infrequently and new employees.

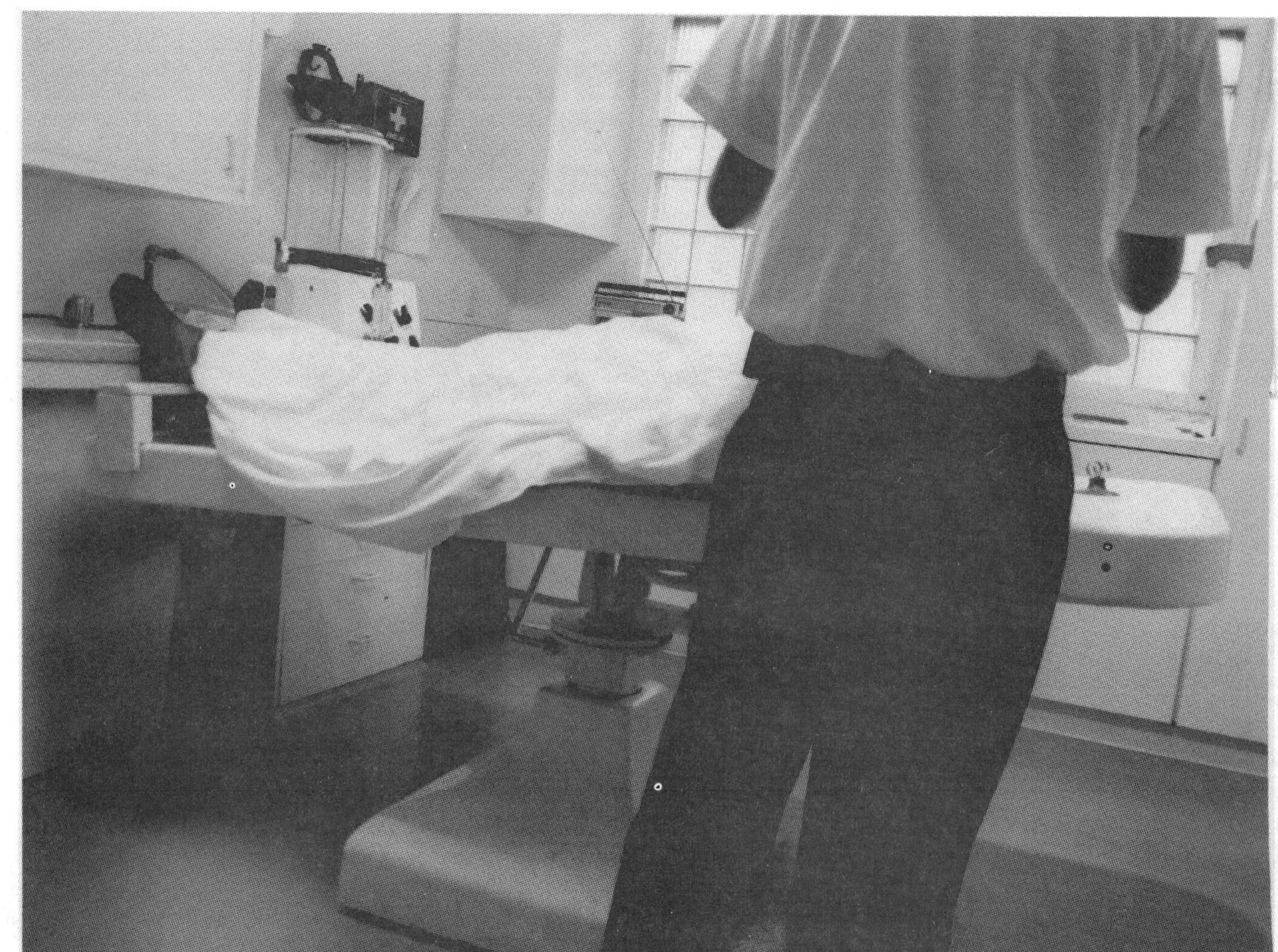

Frequently I walk in to the most
intense situation that most people
will ever experience. One that
everyone will. Usually families in
suburban Gresham. Upper class
homes. short clean rugs. double
car garage. The body is usually in
the basement, the TV room. All the
eyes of the family warm and redden
my ears. S o b e r. I am
absolutely sober. I want so badly
for this to go smoothly. The man
taking charge of the situation talks
to us. Brother, Cousin, friend,
son. Dispensing the necessary
information flatly. Few
transactions or exchanges of
information go so raw and smoothly.
Its easy to turn off at this point.
To go on auto-pilot. To sheet the
body and simply go through the
motions. Rely on the help of your
partner. Making jokes and screwing
around seems so wrong. There aren't
many ways to deal with stinking,
wet, moaning dead people. I'm always
surprised the beloved actually moves
and slides onto the removal cot.
The feeling of plastic over body
sliding, centering the body on the
cot, snap the torso and leg safety
belts, zipping up the car seat
upholstery bag.
        The clicking aluminum cot
pushing back clean carpet, over
doorway, rattling over gray cement
driveways. Then the two thuds as
the cot slides into the mini-van.

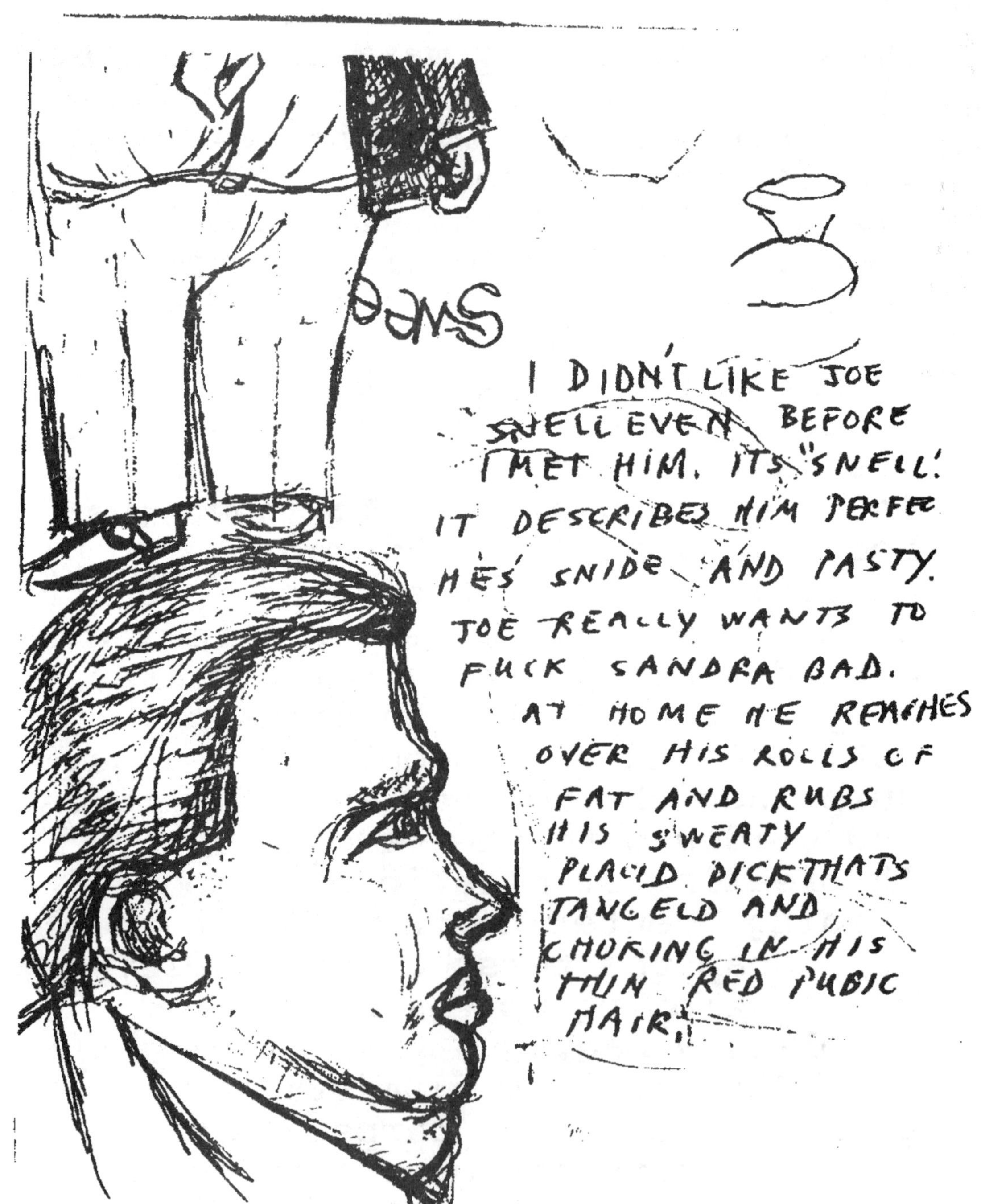

I DIDN'T LIKE JOE
SNELL EVEN BEFORE
I MET HIM. ITS "SNELL!"
IT DESCRIBES HIM PERFE
HE'S SNIDE AND PASTY.
JOE REALLY WANTS TO
FUCK SANDRA BAD.
AT HOME HE REACHES
OVER HIS ROLLS OF
FAT AND RUBS
HIS SWEATY
PLACID DICK THAT'S
TANGELD AND
CHOKING IN HIS
THIN RED PUBIC
HAIR.

JOE SNELL REALLY LIKES SANDRA A LOT. WHO CAN BLAME HIM. SHE DRIVES EVERYONE CRAZY. SHE DROVE ERIN OVER THE EDGE. I THINK ITS HER EYES. JOE BUYS SANDRA FOOD TO SHOW HER HOW MUCH HE CARES. THE THING IS SANDRA THINKS FAT PEOPLE ARE DISGUSTING. WHEN HER AND DAN WERE GOING ON REMOVALS SHE WOULD POINT OUT FAT PEOPLE, "HOW DID THEY LET THEMSELVES GET LIKE THAT." JOE TOOK SANDRA OUT TO TONY ROMA'S THE OTHER NIGHT AND BOUGHT HER RIBS. HE SPENT 30 BUCKS ON THEIR DINNER. TODAY WHEN DAN AND I RELIEVED SANDRA AND JOE OF THEIR SHIFT THERE WAS A NEARLY FULL BOX OF DUNKIN' DONUTS HERE. JOE HAD BOUGHT THE DONUTS, WHEN HE RELIZED THAT SANDRA THOUGHT DONUTS WERE FAT PEOPLE EATING PROBLEM FOOD HE MUST OF QUIT EATING THEM. ILL BET SANDRA DIDN'T EVEN TOUCH ONE. JOE PROBABLY FELT REALLY SHITTY ABOUT BUYING SUCH A HUGE BOX OF DONUTS. IT WAS REALLY FAR TOO MANY. I ATE FIVE TODAY AND DAN ATE THREE. THERE ARE STILL THREE LEFT.

AT FIRST JOE GAVE ME THE CREEPS. BUT I DON'T THINK JOE WANTS PEOPLE TO LIKE HIM. JOE DOES SCARY IMPRESSIONS OF MONTY PYTHON. JOES CAR WAS BROKEN INTO AND WAS NEARLY STOLEN ONE NIGHT WHILE HE WAS AT WORK. "THOSE SHIT HEADS DIDN'T KNOW HOW TO HOT WIRE A CRYSTLER. WHAT THOSE SHIT HEADS DIDN'T KNOW WAS, THAT ON A CRYSTLER YOU NEED TO STICK A PIECE METAL INTO THE IGNITION ALONG WITH THE WIRE," THEN JOE CONTINUED TO TELL US THE CORRECT WAY TO HOT WIRE. SOME OF THE THINGS I SAID ABOUT JOE PROBABLY AREN'T TRUE. THEY WERE JUST IMPRESSIONS.

MY WORST CALL YESTERDAY WAS TO
A REST HOME SOUTH OF TOWN IN CANBY,
THE PLACE STUNK OF URINE AND AMONIA.
THERE WERE OLD PEOPLE IN WHEEL CHAIRS SLOWLY
MOVING UP AND DOWN THE DULL LANOLIUM
FLOORS, PULLING THEMSELVES ALONG WITH THEIR
LEGS, THE LADY WE PICKED UP MUST HAVE BEEN
CRAZY OR SOMETHING, THEY HAD HERE IN A
CORNER OF A ROOM SECTIONED OFF W/ CURTAIN
ON THE FLOOR THERE
WAS A THICK MAT,

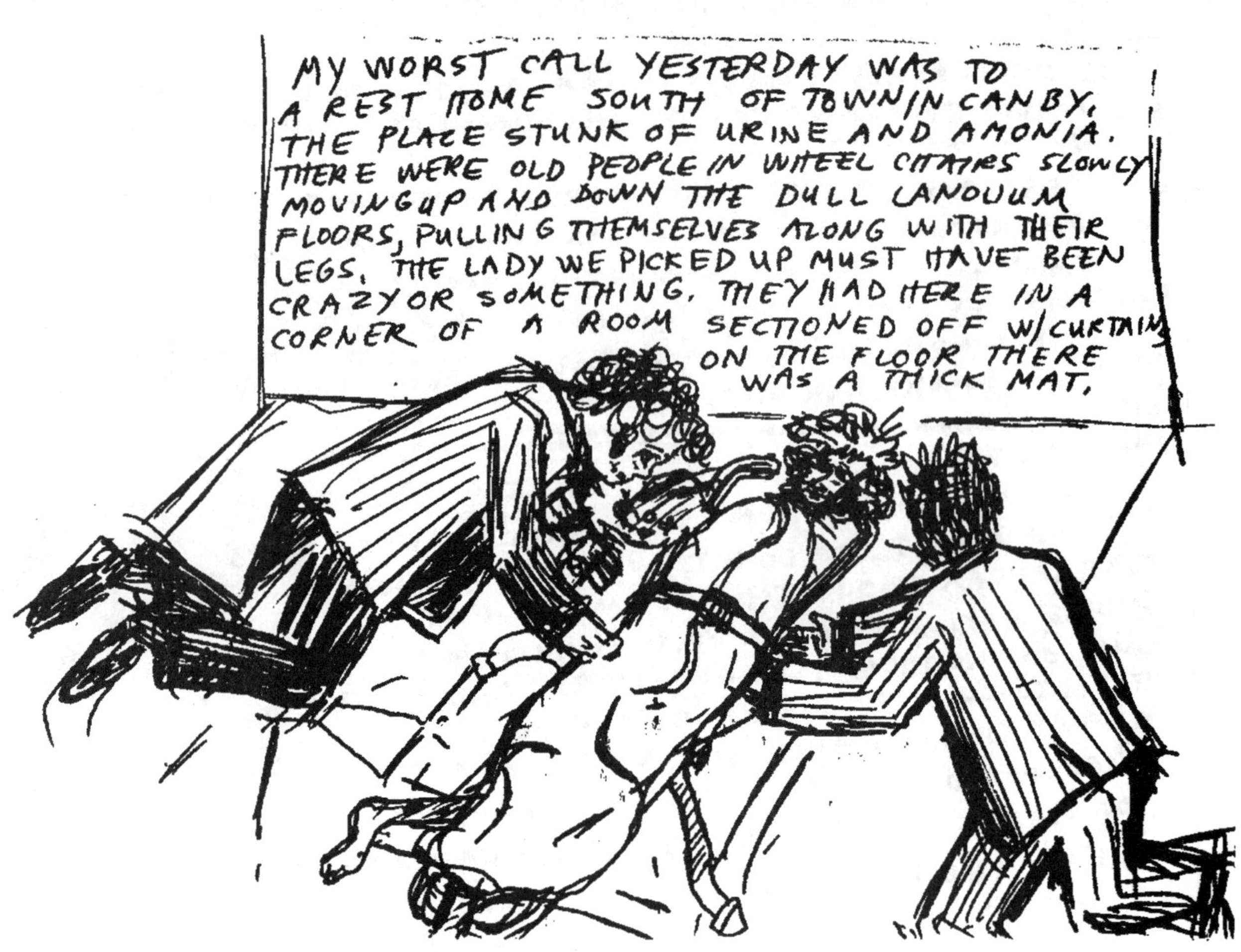

i REALLY WISHED THEY HAD TAKEN HER FORMER ROOM-MATE
OUT WHILE WE WERE REMOVING THE BODY, INSTEAD THEY
HAD HER IN A WHEEL CHAIR ON THE OTHER SIDE OF THE CURTAIN
FACING THE WALL, WE HAD TO USE THE 'SCOOP' OR 'CLAM SHELL'
TO GET HER OFF THE MATS AND ONTO OUR CART. THE SCOOP
IS LIKE A METAL COT THAT DISCONECTS DOWN THE MIDDLE,
YOU PLACE ONE HALF ON EACH SIDE OF THE BELOVED AND
RE-CONNECT THE HALVES UNDER THE BODY. THEN ITS EASY
TO PICK THEM UP. BUT WE WERE NERVOUS AND HADN'T
USED THE 'SCOOP.' WHEN WE MOVED HER TO PLACE A SHEET
AROUND HER GAS CAME OUT. SHE   LET OUT A
SMALL MOAN AND SMELLED   LIKE SHIT
AND OUR LATEX GLOVES,   WE STARTED
TO HURRY AND KEPT   ACCIDENTLY
KNOCKING HER HEAD   AND HER
TIRED MATTED   GREY
HAIR KEPT   GETTING
CAUGHT   IN THE
CROME   CLAMP
OF THE   'SCOOP.'

Our office is approximately fifteen by fifteen feet. There are two grey metal cabinets. There are two desks that face each other and at each desk is a swivel chair on rollers. Both desks contain various office supplies, and the carpet around the desks is covered by clear plastic in order to facillitate the movement of the chairs. Each desk has a phone. My desk has a typewrtiter and Alex's has three phone books. In one corner there is a small artificial wood cabinet that has supplies for making coffee, and sitting on top of that is a coffee maker and a brown paper bag with six coffee cups. My cup says Sunsoft in blue print. There are three windows that provide a view of a wood fence. A lamp post stands by both desks. The bulbs in the lamps are uncovered and have three settings that provide a slight gradation in the brightness of life. There is a straight back wooden chair sitting by the door way. A T.V. with a built in VCR sits facing the wall on another wooden chair. A metal folding chair leans against the wall next to the coffee table.

A beige heater and beige waste basket are in opposite corners. On an average day we will spend four to six hours in the office.

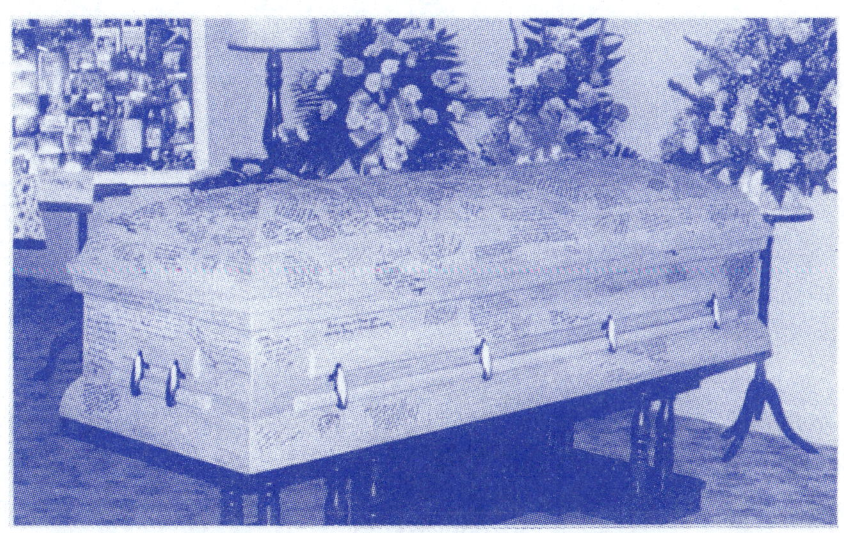

Barry Dillinger's Story

I think it was during my second or third week as a removal technician that I had the opportunity to work with Barry Dillinger. I worked the midnight to eight shift that night, and although we only had one removal, I learned a lot. For awhile Barry was sort of my removal technician hero. He just has a real special kind of attitude that's perfect for making removals. The funeral industry seems to be divided between people who mainly handle the arrangement of funerals and that sort of thing on one hand, and people who spend most of their time away from the public embalming and making removals on the other. It's not that Barry is anti-social or uncharismatic, but he definitely falls into the second category of funeral workers.

When I asked Barry about how he ended up in this line of work, he just leaned back in his chair and laughed (Barry has snaggly crooked teeth that are only visible when he laughs). Barry grew up in a small town in Virginia across the street from a funeral home. On pale blue sunny days he would ride his bike through the parking lot. At that time Barry was vaguely aware of a man working at the funeral home named Mr. Thompson. Probably the only thing Barry knew about Mr. Thompson was that he wore a suit and he did something with bodies.

Barry's family moved to a new home when Barry was about six, but this was only the beginning of his relationship with Mr. Thompson. Mr. Thompson was Barry's third grade basketball coach, and sixth grade math teacher. They became closer to each other, and Mr. Thompson became a sort of father figure for Barry. Barry learned that Mr. Thompson made removals for extra money in his spare time.

When Barry was seventeen Mr. Thompson died, and Barry was asked to be a pall bearer at his funeral. Only a few days after the funeral, Barry got a call from the local funeral director who offered Barry Mr. Thompson's position. This was an incredible honor and Barry wasted no time in snatching up the opportunity. So, during Barry's senior year of high school, his after school job consisted of picking up dead bodies. After a couple months Barry knew that this is what he wanted to do with his life. He spent five years in the army, and as soon as he got out he was right back into the funeral business.

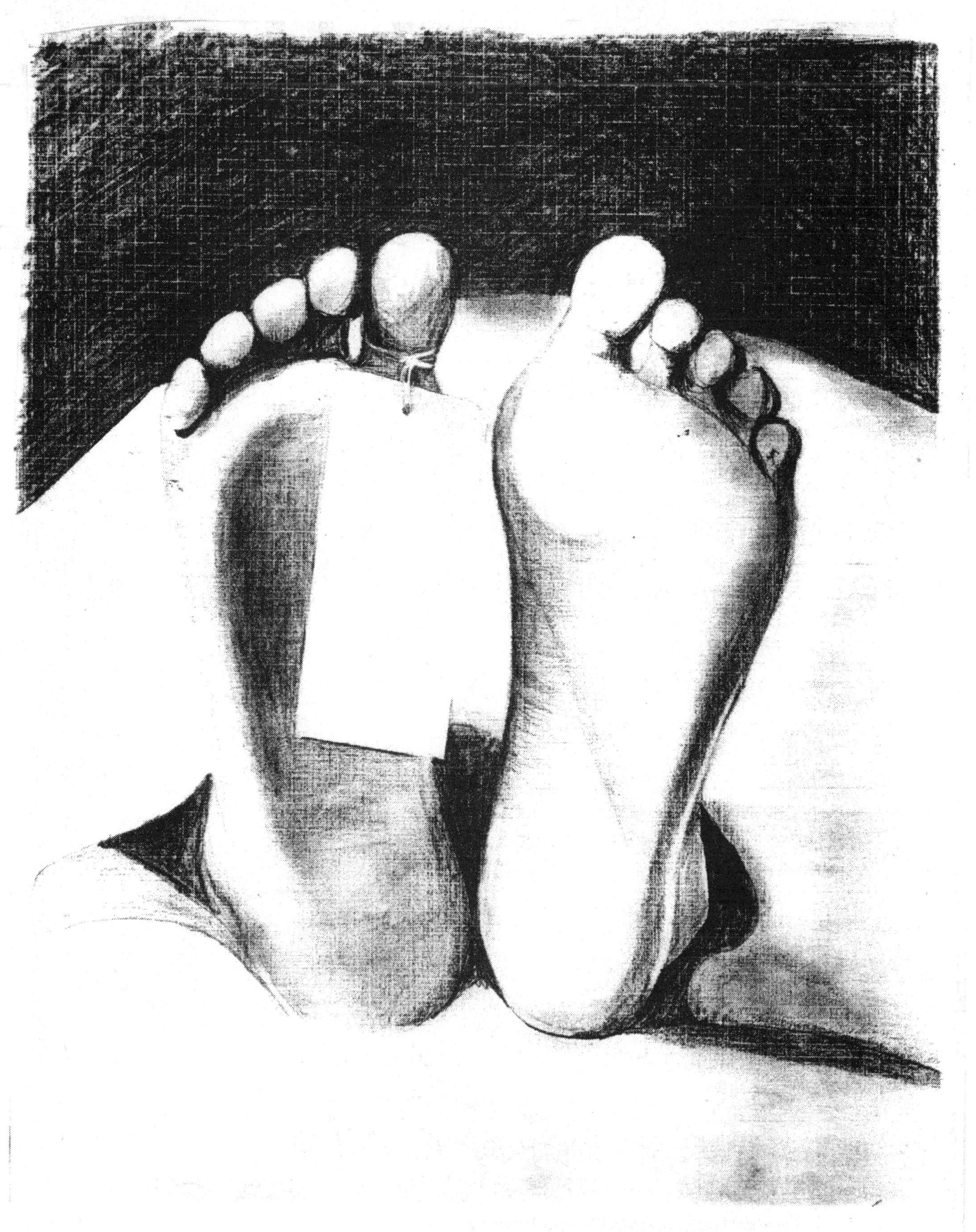

Drawing By Elizabeth Hubbard
(Alexs Mother)

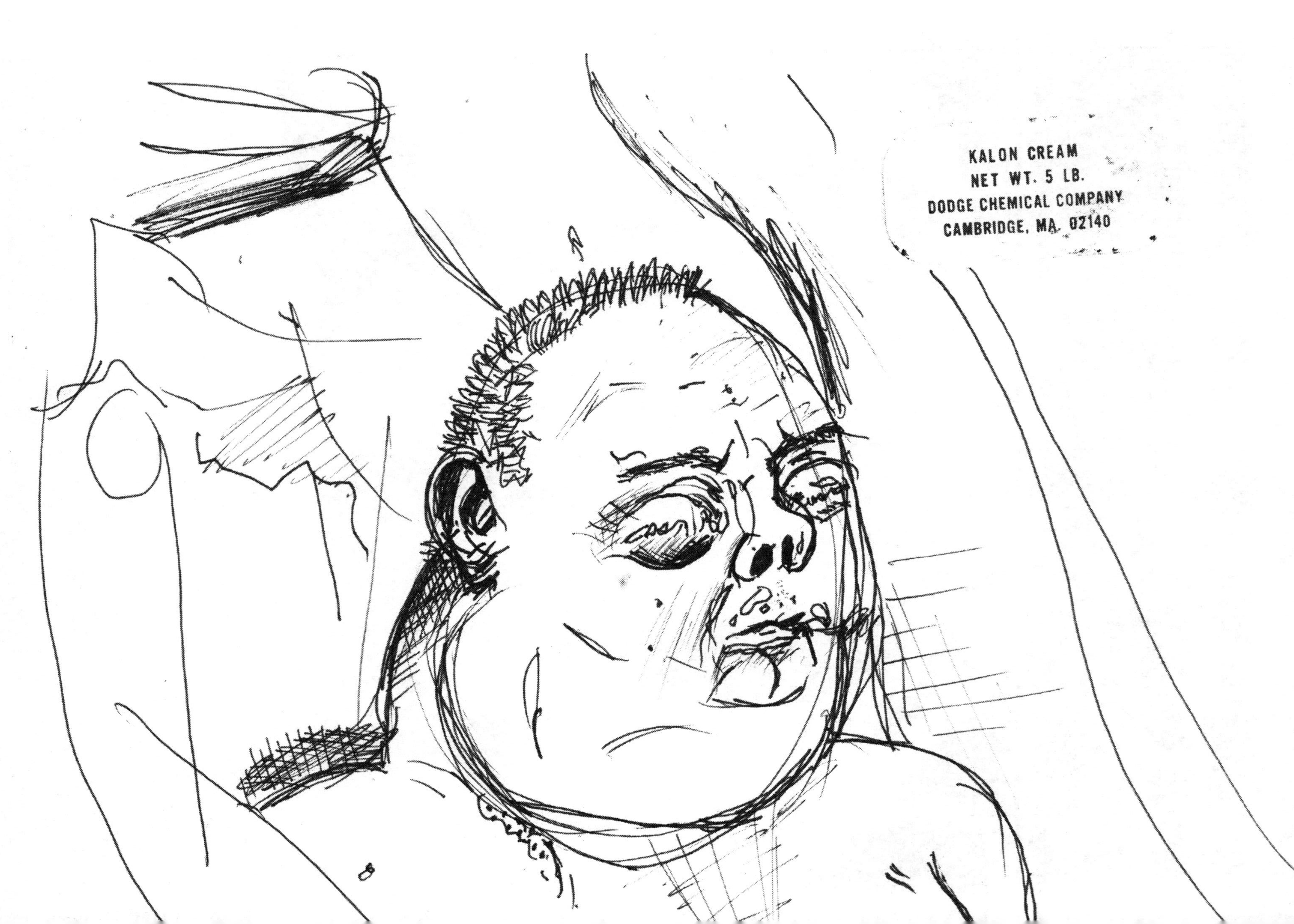

KALON CREAM
NET WT. 5 LB.
DODGE CHEMICAL COMPANY
CAMBRIDGE, MA. 02140

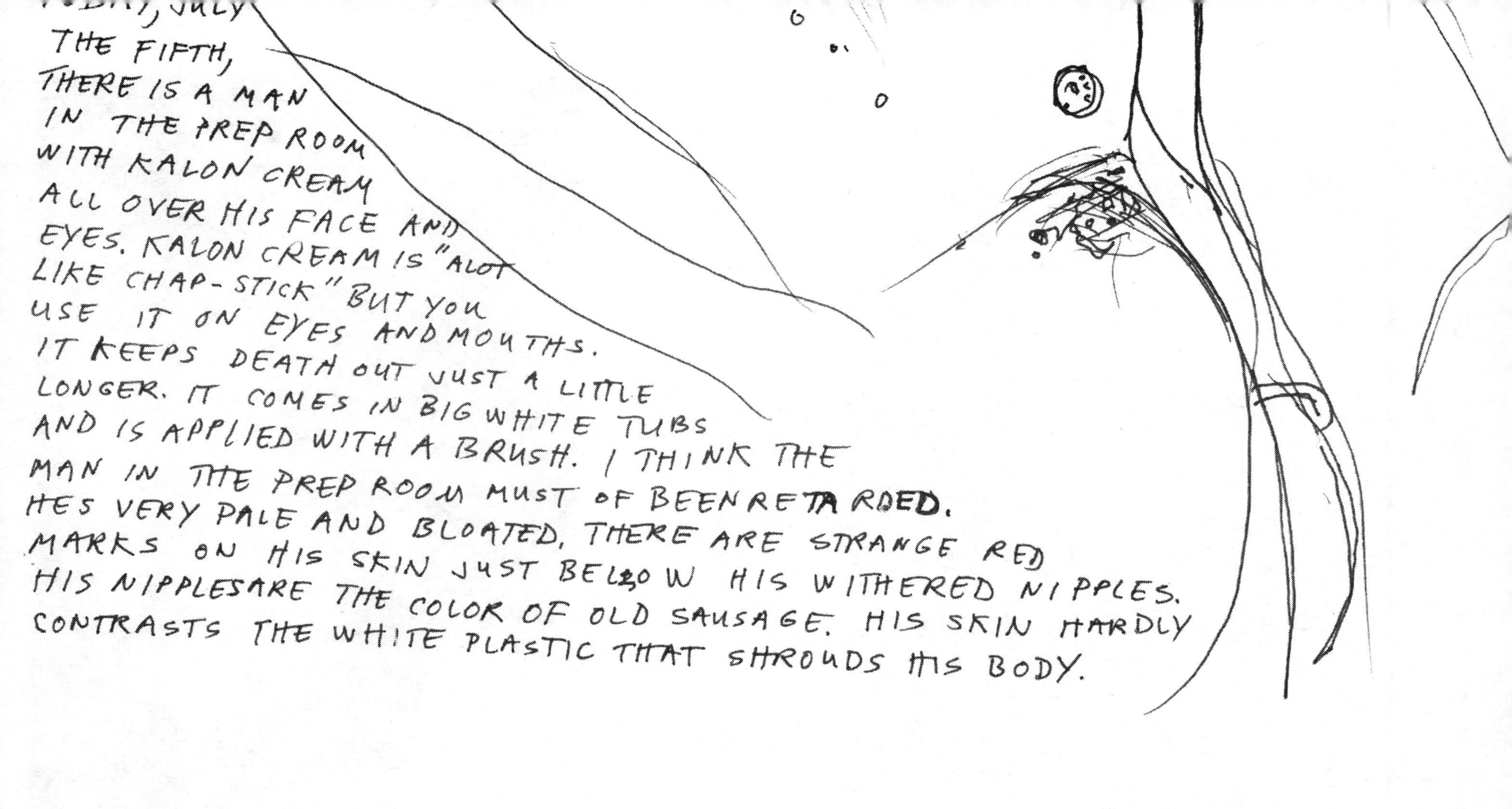

TODAY, JULY
THE FIFTH,
THERE IS A MAN
IN THE PREP ROOM
WITH KALON CREAM
ALL OVER HIS FACE AND
EYES. KALON CREAM IS "ALOT
LIKE CHAP-STICK" BUT YOU
USE IT ON EYES AND MOUTHS.
IT KEEPS DEATH OUT JUST A LITTLE
LONGER. IT COMES IN BIG WHITE TUBS
AND IS APPLIED WITH A BRUSH. I THINK THE
MAN IN THE PREP ROOM MUST OF BEEN RETARDED.
HE'S VERY PALE AND BLOATED. THERE ARE STRANGE RED
MARKS ON HIS SKIN JUST BELOW HIS WITHERED NIPPLES.
HIS NIPPLES ARE THE COLOR OF OLD SAUSAGE. HIS SKIN HARDLY
CONTRASTS THE WHITE PLASTIC THAT SHROUDS HIS BODY.

embalm-according to Barry the only difficult thing about embalming is locating the juggler vein. Once you've found that you pretty much just replace the deceased's blood with embalming fluid. Some people think that certain organs are removed, but this really isn't true. The longer a body sits in the cooler the more difficult it is to embalm. The blood tends to quagulate, and will occaisonally require a six point incision in order to complete the embalming. Once a person is embalmed they really don't need to be stored in a cooler anymore. The embalming fluid will keep them fresh. An embalmed body takes on a waxy look. In some ways an embalmed person looks more dead then a non embalmed person. A regular body will have it's mouth all twisted up and really just looks like it's sleeping. Bill Briscoe is a good embalmer. I overheard the directors over at Bateman's taking a look at a forty eight year old man that Bill had embalmed (they weren't at all disturbed by his naked deadness), quietly saying to each that "Bill does good work". They said it in a self assured way that sort of implied that it would be very surprising to run into a poorly embalmed body that Bill was responsible for. Today Bill dressed an older woman that he had probably embalmed sometime in the last couple days. He wore blue rubber gloves and and a plastic smock. Bill always seems much more confident when he's wearing his blue rubber embalming gloves.

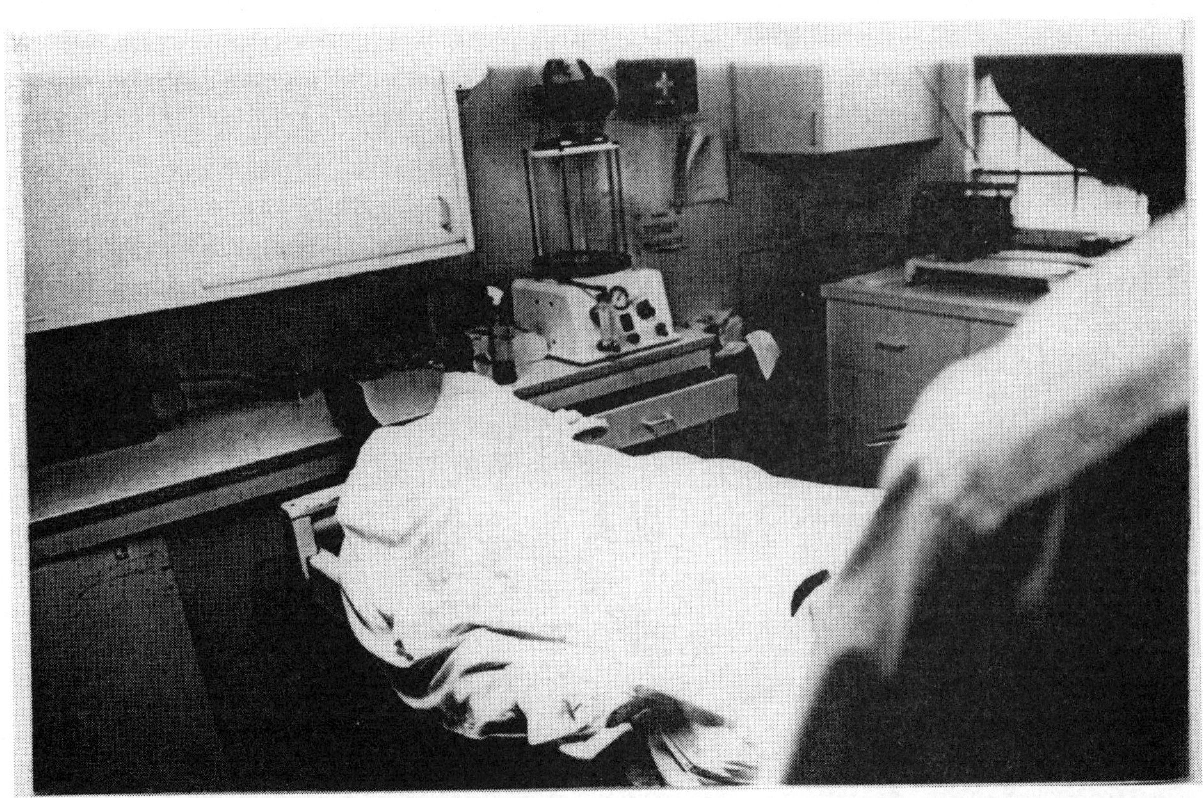

19 Ways to Help the Grieving

When Dan and Alex walk up to the door of someone's home to remove their husband (so far it's always been a husband) they're usually a little bit nervous and they adjust their ties in the reflection off the window of the van. They both wear dark suits. Dan wears a white shirt with a thin red tie and Alex wears a blue shirt with a blue and brown striped tie. Dan knocks on the door and introduces Alex and himself. Whoever answers the door has been crying and Dan talks to them in a barely audible voice explaining that they need a few pieces of information before they can remove the body. The family never knows his social security number and sometimes they have to fish his wallet out of his pants.

There's always someone watching them remove the body and they usually end up helping. For some reason Dan and Alex can never seem to get the body from the bed to the cot as easily when they're in a home as they can at a hospital. Sometimes one of them will end up kneeling on the bed trying to shove the body. Dan and Alex aren't completely comfortable with touching the bodies, and it's not unusual for them to only pretend to be trying to move the body, while the family does the real work.

Dan generally gets the information from the family, and Alex talks them through the actual removal, but neither of them know exactly what to say when they are leaving. There's a tendency to want to say I'm Sorry or Thank You, but neither of these is appropriate. Once when Dan was still working with Jason, the wife apologized because her husband had been so difficult to remove. She was crying and Dan couldn't speak. He had blood on his shirt sleeve and he was soaked in sweat. It was horrible.

Glenn Dixon is the lowest on the totem
pole of funeral directors here at
Gables. Glenn smokes Dorals and he
has a sort of a low gravely (actually
more sandy then gravely) voice. For
some reason when I answer the phone
people always think it's Glenn, so I
guess I must sound a little bit like
him. Glenn hates his job and uses
words like "shit fit", as in, "When
management sees all this overtime I'm
getting they're going to throw a shit
fit". Today Glenn sat down on a desk
rubbed his eyes, sighed and said "I
don't know why I got into this fucking
line of work." He just had gotten off
the phone with some "price choppers"
who were calling around to all the
different funeral services to find the
best price for the disposal of their
beloved. Glenn is the only one of the
directors that I'm relatively confident
that he doesn't do strange things to
the bodies. It seems like if he was
fucking dead people he would probably
enjoy his job a little more. I also
don't think Glenn is a very good embalmer.

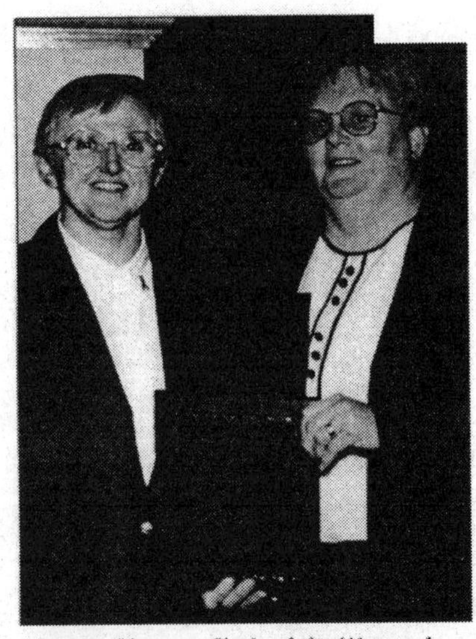

*Mary K. Gleason, Chair of the Women in
Funeral Service Advisory Committee (left)
congratulates Funeral Service Woman of
the Year Laura Zabel.*

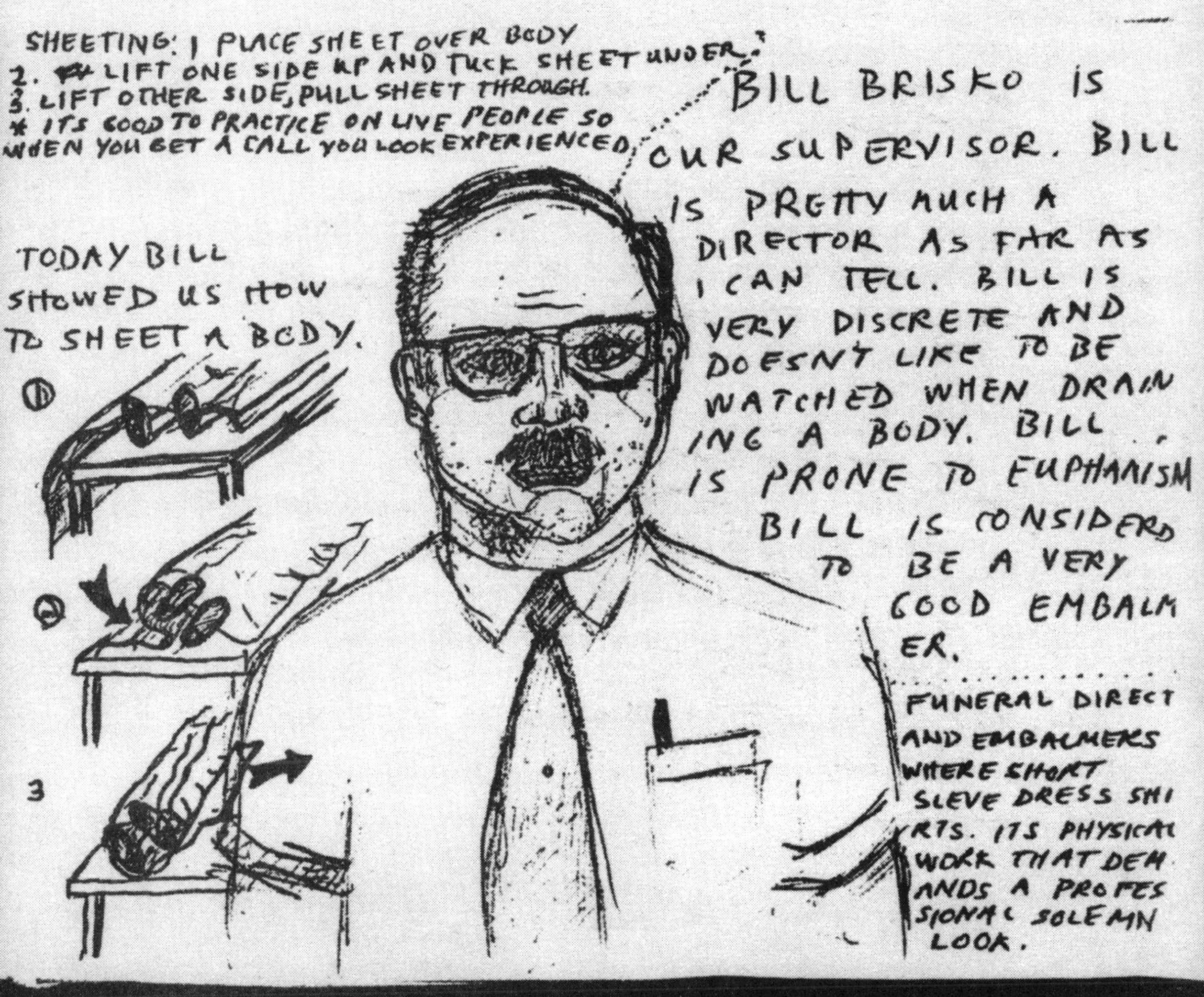

SHEETING: 1 PLACE SHEET OVER BODY
2. LIFT ONE SIDE UP AND TUCK SHEET UNDER.
3. LIFT OTHER SIDE, PULL SHEET THROUGH.
* ITS GOOD TO PRACTICE ON LIVE PEOPLE SO
WHEN YOU GET A CALL YOU LOOK EXPERIENCED.

TODAY BILL
SHOWED US HOW
TO SHEET A BODY.
1
2
3

BILL BRISKO IS
OUR SUPERVISOR. BILL
IS PRETTY MUCH A
DIRECTOR AS FAR AS
I CAN TELL. BILL IS
VERY DISCRETE AND
DOESN'T LIKE TO BE
WATCHED WHEN DRAIN
ING A BODY. BILL
IS PRONE TO EUPHANISM
BILL IS CONSIDERD
TO BE A VERY
GOOD EMBALM
ER.

FUNERAL DIRECT
AND EMBALMERS
WHERE SHORT
SLEVE DRESS SHI
RTS. ITS PHYSICAL
WORK THAT DEM
ANDS A PROFES
SIONAL SOLEMN
LOOK.

PEAKS FUNERAL HOME
IS LOCATED IN MILWAUKE
OREGON AND IS OPERATED
BY DALE SEIPES.

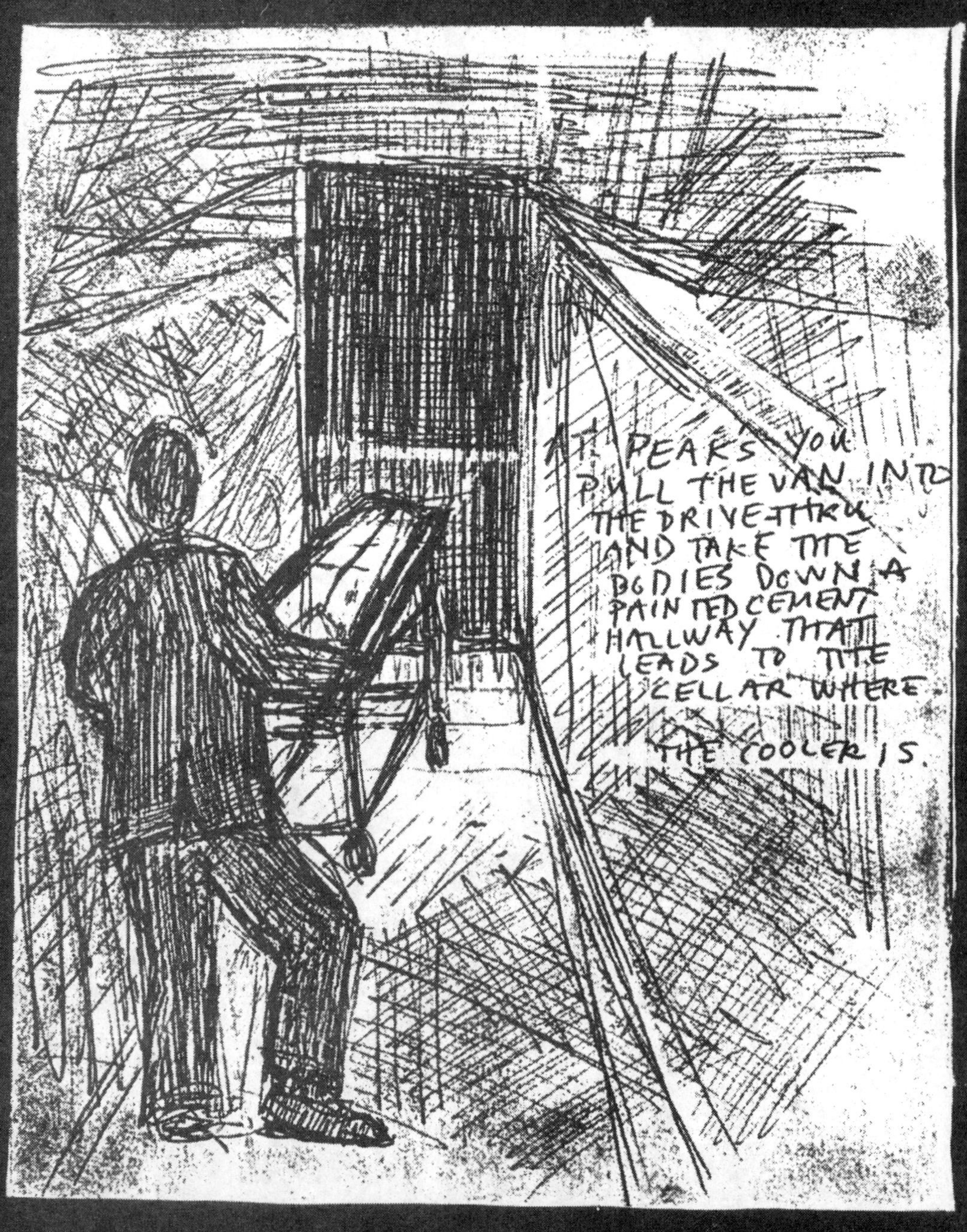

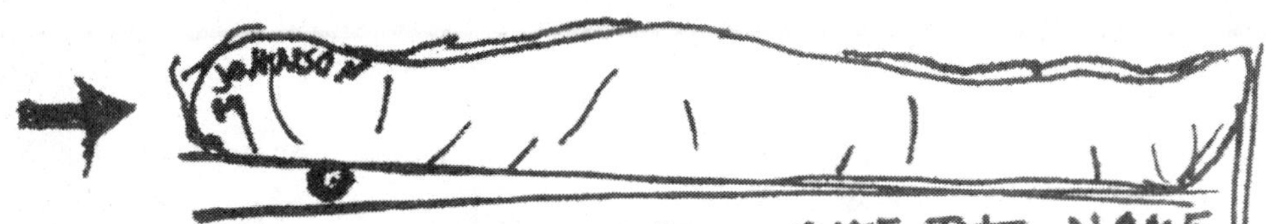

* ITS VERY IMPORTANT TO WRITE THE NAME OF THE BODY ON THE OUTSIDE OF THE PLASTIC, BY THE HEAD. OTHERWISE DALE WOULD HAVE TO SLIDE THE BODY OUT TO SEE WHO IT WAS.

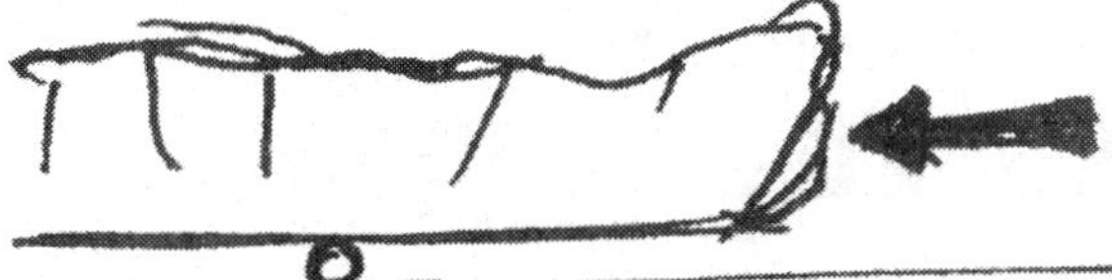

HEAD BLOCKS ARE ALWAYS TO BE USED AT PEAKS

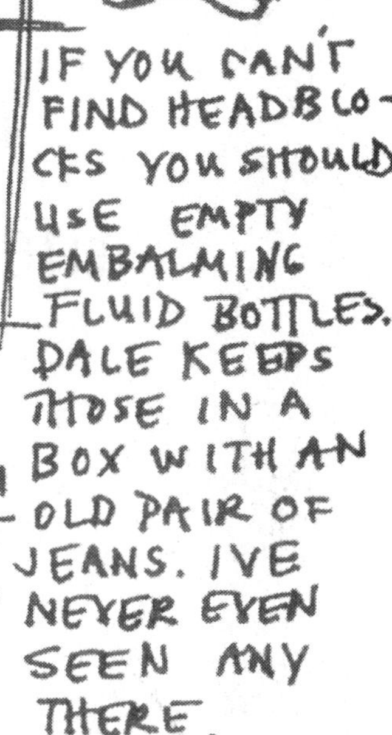

IF YOU CAN'T FIND HEADBLO- CKS YOU SHOULD USE EMPTY EMBALMING FLUID BOTTLES. DALE KEEPS THOSE IN A BOX WITH AN OLD PAIR OF JEANS. IVE NEVER EVEN SEEN ANY THERE.

AT PEAKS THERE IS A VERY SPECIFIC ~~THIS IS~~ PROCEDURE TO FOLLOW. AS BILL SAYS, "IF YOU DO SOMETHING WRONG, DALE WILL LET HIM KNOW." BILL SAYS DALE IS PICKY. BODIES AT PEAKS ARE LIFTED WITH A HYDROLIC LIFT AND THEN ROLLED ONTO A PIECE OF DOWLING WHICH THEN ROLLS THE BODY, WHICH IS ON A PIECE OF PLYWOOD, INTO THE SHELF. DALE LIKES THE BODIES HANDS TO BE SUPPORTED OR AT LEAST CROSSED ON THEIR CHESTS.

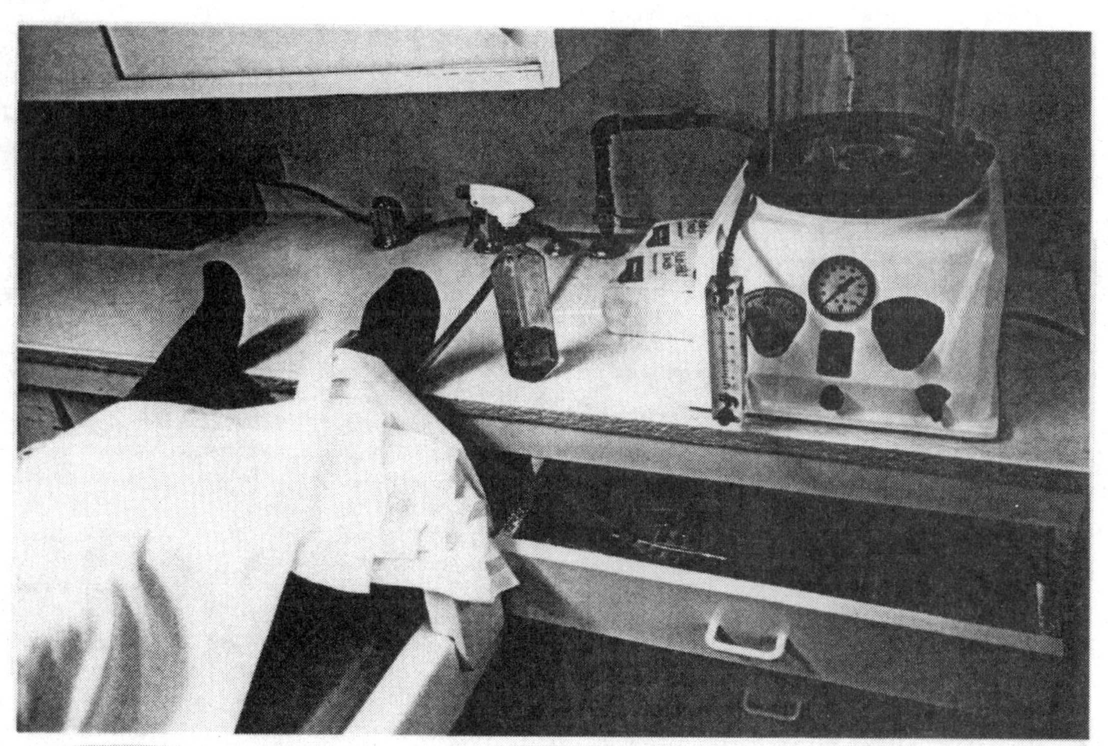

STEPHEN R. KEMP

Solutions to Embalming the Intravenous Drug Abuser

The intravenous drug abuser presents the embalmer/funeral director with a myriad of problems associated with the recreational injection of drugs. This article will address the various embalming problems associated with drug abusers and how to solve them.

Infective endocarditis

One of the most common complications in the intravenous drug abuser (IVDA) is the presence of endocarditis. Infective endocarditis is the presence of vegetative organisms on the cardiac valves of infected patients.

The most common causative organism is .S. *Aureus* in IVDA patients. This organism along with other microorganisms can infect a patient and at times present a polymicrobial generalized infection with histoplasma, saccharomyces, cryptococcus, candida and other opportunistic organisms. Infection of the left side of the heart is often seen, however, infection of the right side is common in IVDA patients.

The common medical and post-mortem complication are, multiple cardiovascular accidents (stroke), herniated brain stem, clubbing of the fingertips, small hemorrhages known as petechiae and irregular flat erythematous lesions known an Janeway lesions. The endocarditis IVDA patient causes not only vascular problems for the embalmer, but also problems with the integument and fluid balance in the final embalming results.

IVDA and the integument

Effective results of the embalming process of the IVDA patient must deal with skin complications of the disease. The injection of opiates, heroin, cocaine and other related recreational drugs can cause an inflammatory response of the integument due to their alkaline states. This complication will present the embalmer with necrosis, multiple abscesses, both infective and sterile, infectious cellulitis of the extremities and multiple punctate lesions in the nailbeds of patients known as petechial hemorrhages.

The embalming of the person with these complications requires a minimum fluid dilution of three percent. The fluid should be of a high index, more than 30. The embalmer needs this index to disinfect, dry and reduce tissue swelling during injection of the primary dilution of embalming fluid. The integument ulcers should be treated with cavity with a high phenol content. One must be cognizant that the skin lesion may be infectious and communicable, often with antibiotic resistant microorganisms that may infect the embalmer.

The most effective treatment for swelling in these cases is careful and methodical massaging of the extremities to reduce fluid deposition in these areas. The limitation of the technique is where the site has been excessively used for injection and had keratinized and thickened to an extent where the damage is unrestorable.

The IVDA patient and vascular considerations

The most crucial and difficult test for the embalmer and the IVDA case is the location, isolation and injection of patent arteries. The IVDA patient when alive is the best phlebotomist and artery locator. Often in emergency situations, the drug user will tell the physician where to start an intravenous or arterial line.

After many years of abuse, the IVDA has very few if any usable veins and arteries to inject. The best method of injecting these cases is to check the entire body for old lesions and scars. These lesions will often occur at the groin, neck, axillaries, dorsum of the hand and anticubital fossa.

If the extremity distal to your possible injection site is darkened or necrotic, do not open the artery. The necrosis is due to a lack of circulation secondary to vegetative organisms, atherosclerosis and emboli, which have migrated from the primary lesion. The best injection site is usually the internal carotid artery. With careful blunt dissection and a minimal incision, the carotid can be opened and injected slowly with a low pressure, two to five pounds initially.

The injection should proceed slowly and observe carefully for the presence of migrating emboli. The presence of patent intravenous lines should be left open during the injection. Also, if there are patent arterial lines in the radial or ulnar arteries, these should be used for the injection of the hands and forearm.

Vigorous induction of drainage is crucial to a successful outcome in embalming these cases; the reasons are multiple loose vegetations from the cardiac valves lodged in the extremities, multiple clots formed by disseminated intravascular coagulation (DIC), a common complication in endocarditis, and multiple adhesions caused by excessive scar tissue.

The injection of vascular complicated cases may be aided with the use of catheters. I use flexible Teflon and/or polyethylene catheters used in vascular surgery and cardiac catheterizations to selectively inject the head and extremities when regular methods fail. The carotid artery may be atrophic and may contain vegetative material from the infected valve. The catheter is very useful in these cases.

The catheter may be inserted under the guidance of a guide wire and moved to various points in the vascular system and give flow to areas that may otherwise go without good circulation. It is especially useful in the injection of hands and clearing of discoloration. Finally, we must consider other considerations in the embalming of IVDA patients, namely presence of other communicable pathogens.

Other considerations

One of the most important Occupational Safety and Health Administration (OSHA) rules is the bloodborne pathogen rule. Especially in an IVDA, the remains have an increased risk of transmission of Hepatitis A, B and non-A, non-B genera. The presence of HIV and opportunistic organisms also are prevalent in these populations. The presence of HIV necessitates the utmost precaution in the preparation of these remains.

The IVDA case again requires the use of at least concentration of two percent and an index of a minimum of 30. In addition, due to stenosis and/or presence of prosthetic valves, the embalmer must use a multi-point injection to ensure thorough distribution of arterial solution. Often body fluid contamination, dilution of edema and renal failure will complicate and retard formaldehyde fixation and preservation. If sepsis is present, the addition of glutaraldehyde is always advisable to ensure proper disinfection.

While embalming the intravenous drug user can present some unique challenges, it is my hope that I have created some awareness of the complications involved and how to approach them. ∎

Stephen Kemp is director and general manager of Stinson Funeral Homes, Detroit, MI, and a staff member of LSC Acquisition Co. He is a former professor at Wayne State University's School of Mortuary Science.

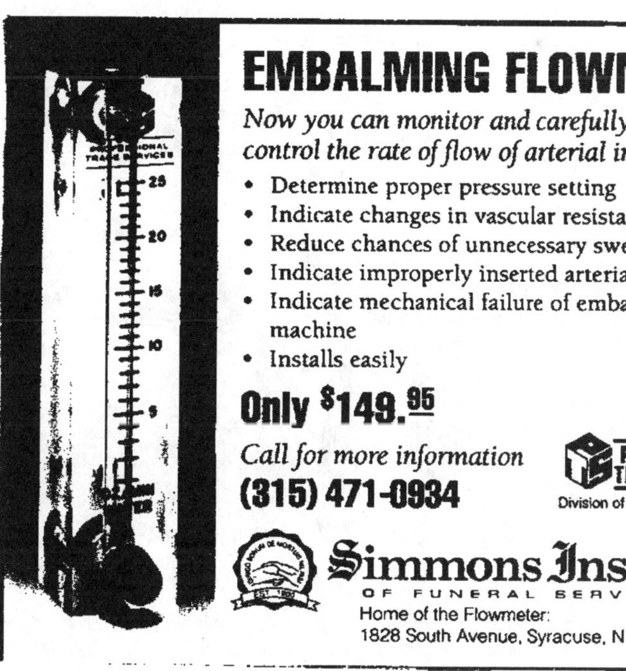

She's slumped over in a wooden chair facing the toilet with dark blood caked around her mouth. It smells like piss. We shut the bathroom door and slide her off the chair and it smells worse, she's cold and stiff, the cop said the time of death was 19:00, but that's not even close. It's hot and we have to put the chair in the bathtub to get her positioned right, everything is so snell and she keeps smelling more and there's piss everywhere and I turn on the fan in the bathroom. I'm momentarily distracted by the feeling of the soles of my shoes balancing on the curved surface of the bathtub. I see myself in slow motion, dressed in a suit, wearing white latex gloves sliding the glass of the shower door. The flourescent bathroom lighting makes my movements so bright and yellow. We're both talking under our breath but all of the sound is sucked up by the fan.

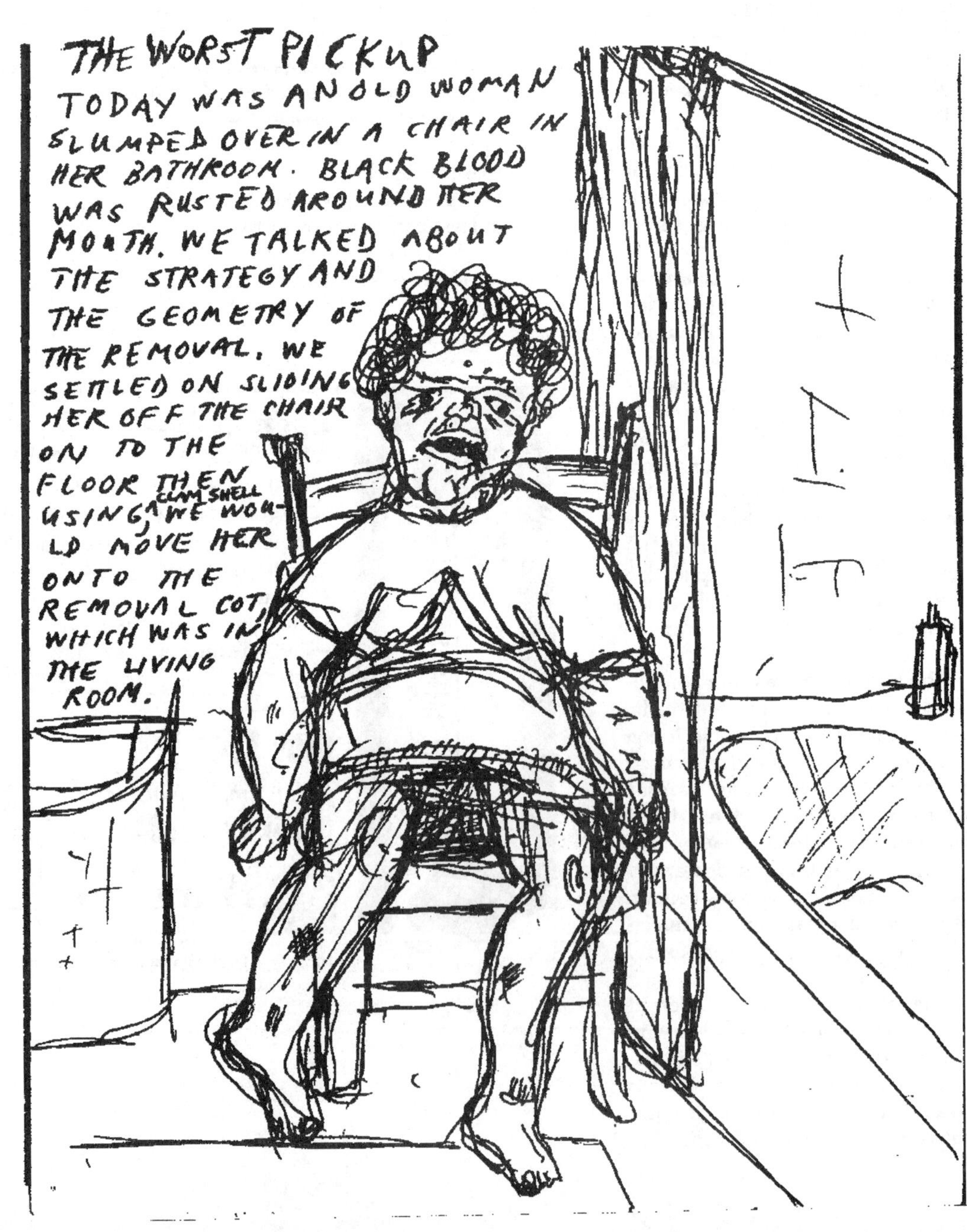

At this point it's all geometry and angles. Her legs are stiff enough that they can only be moved in certain directions. Right now they're spread on either side of the toilet and we need to get them together if we're going to move them. I guess her legs aren't much bigger then mine, but their bloated yellow smoothness makes her seem huge. I wrap both hands around her right calf and move it to the left side of the toilet. This allows us to rotate the body so the head is near the door and her legs are laying straight out on the floor. she's in the bathroom dead, slumped over in a wooden chair with dark blood crusted around her mouth. Someone says that she said she was ready to die. We realize that she's too close to the door and Alex has to lift her body out of the way in order for me to get the door open. There's not enough clearance and the door is catching on her dress and Alex grabs her with both hands and I push the door hard and gasp and there's sweat beading on my forehead.

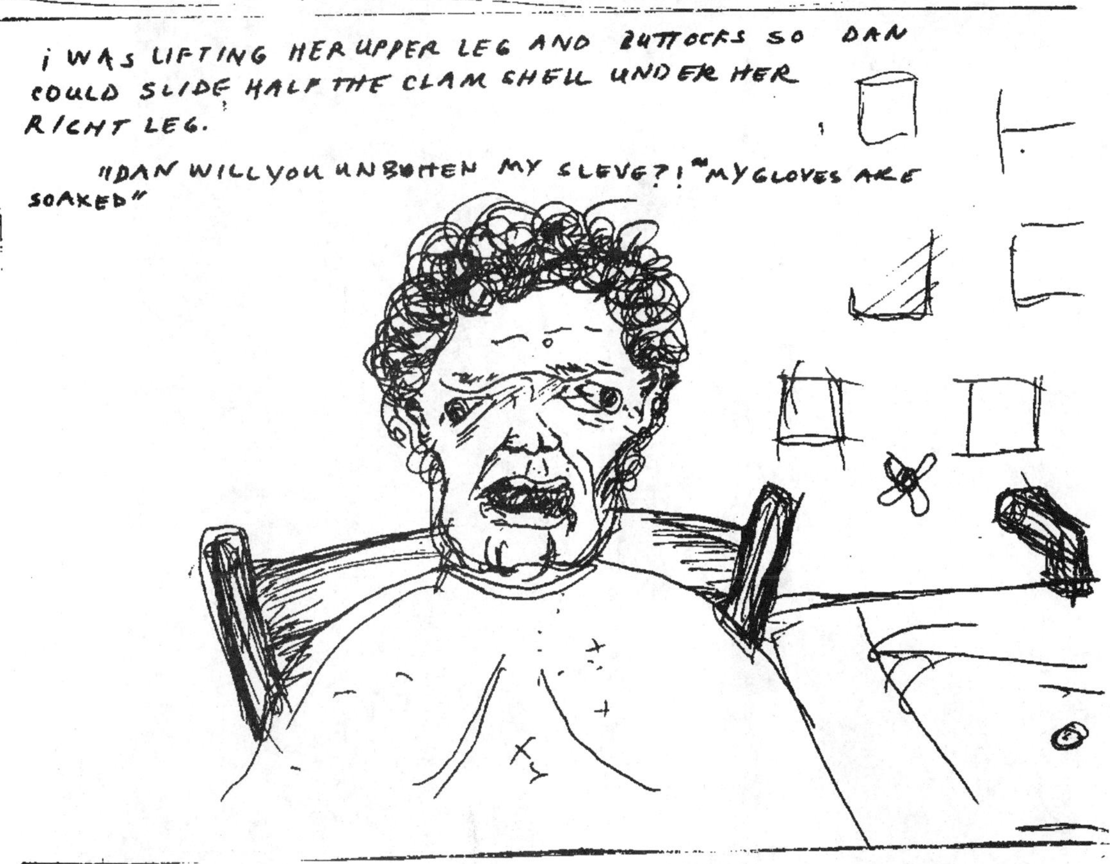

The clamp shell is a tool designed for removing a body from a place where the cot won't fit. It's an aluminum oval connected by three scoops on either side. We dismantle the clamp shell and place half on either side of her. Alex lifts the body while I slide the shell under her back. It's difficult to avoid pinching her flesh between the scoops.

Alex takes the head and I take the feet. We carry her to the removal cot. Someone from the family burns sage and it smells like weed and we ache and we zip the bag around her but we leave the face showing. Does anyone want the face showing?

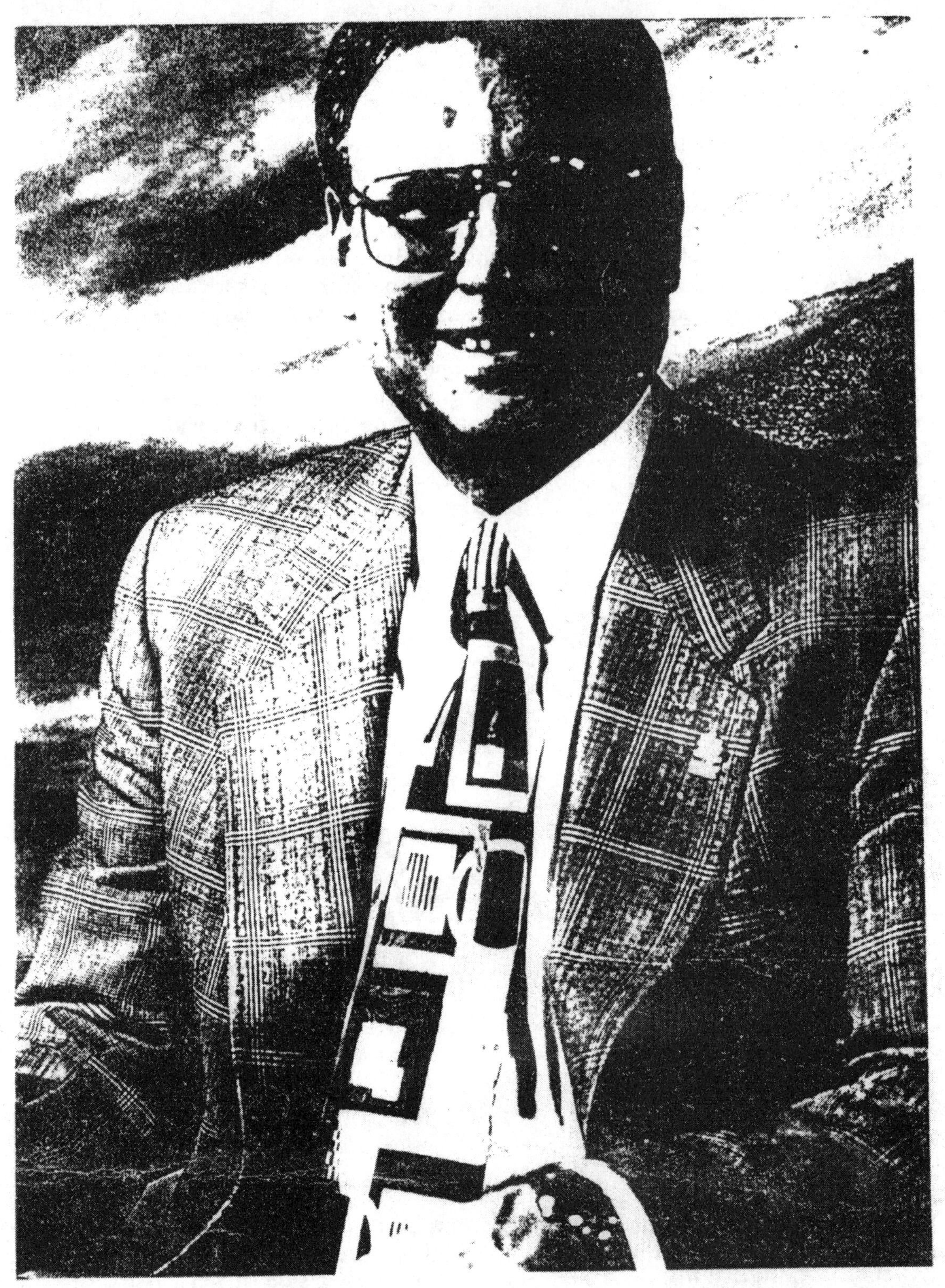

PLEASE SEND QUESTIONS,
COMMENTS, STORIES, OR ANYTHING
ELSE ie HAIR CLIPPINGS OR FINGER
NAILS TO The Removal Technician
LC Box 727
PORTLAND, OR. 97219

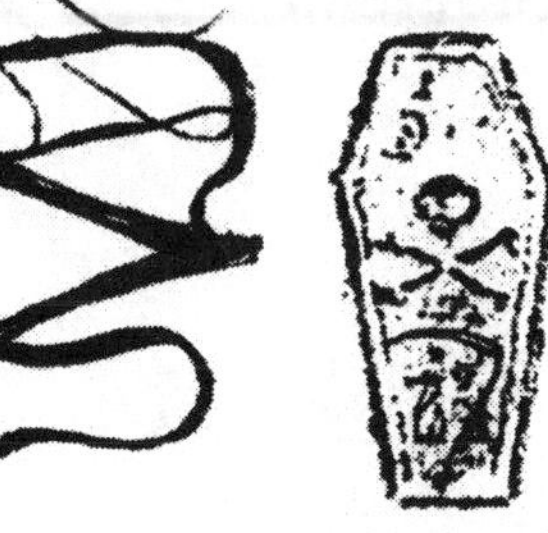
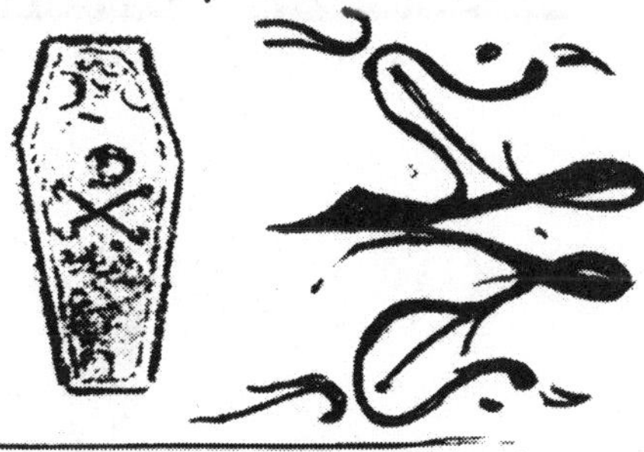

THE REMOVAL TECHNICIAN

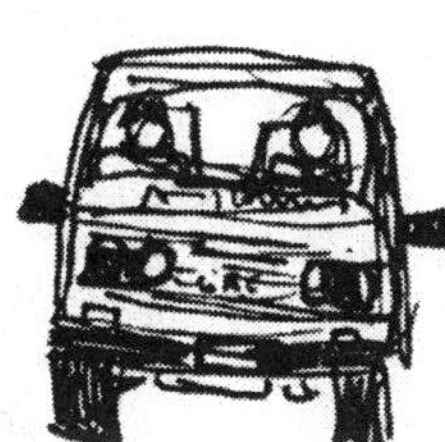

ISSUE TWO

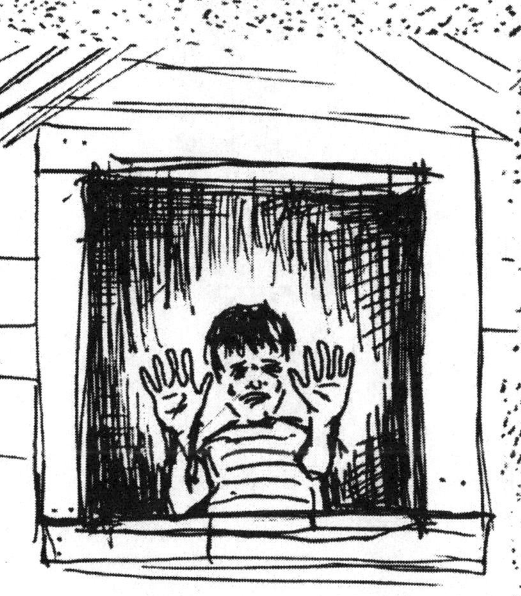

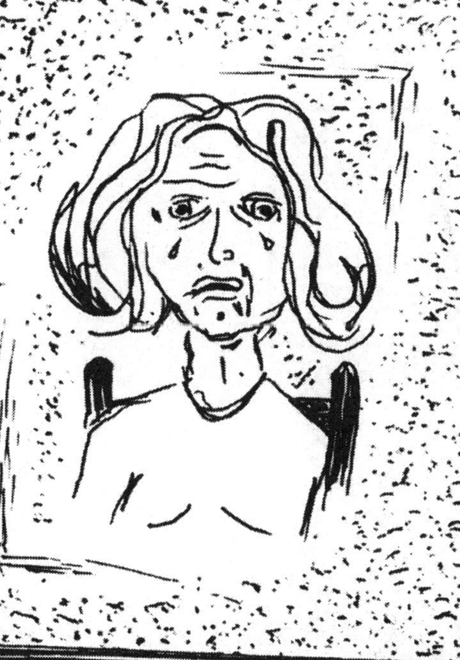

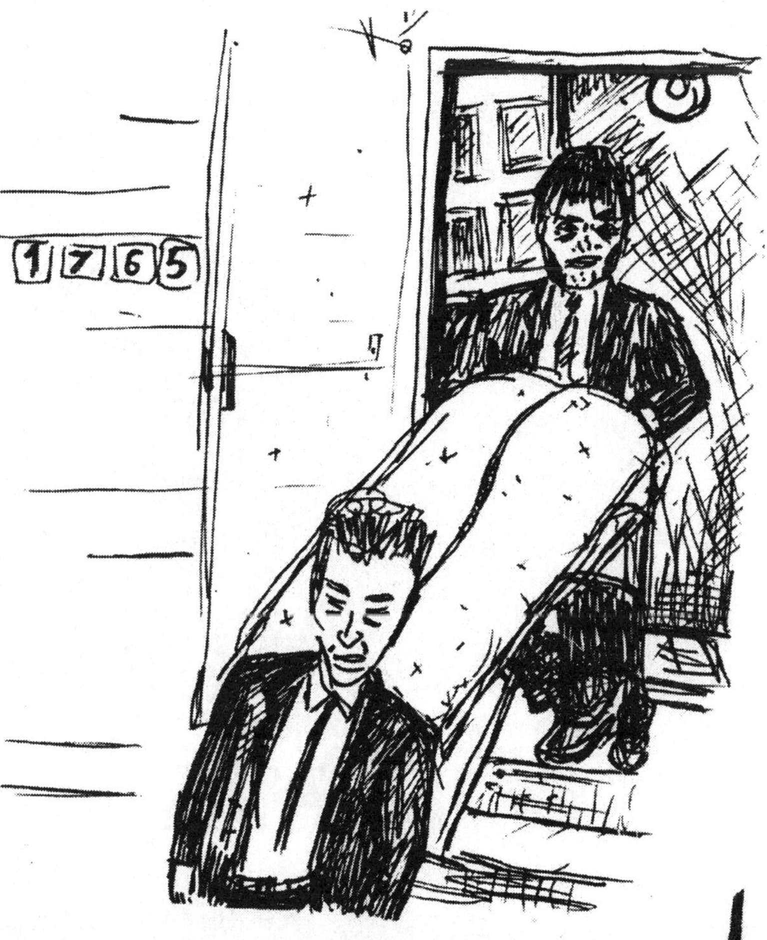

Editorial Note: Many of the characters featured in issue #2 were introduced in issue #1. In order to fully enjoy The Removal Technician, we highly reccomend that you read or reread issue #1.

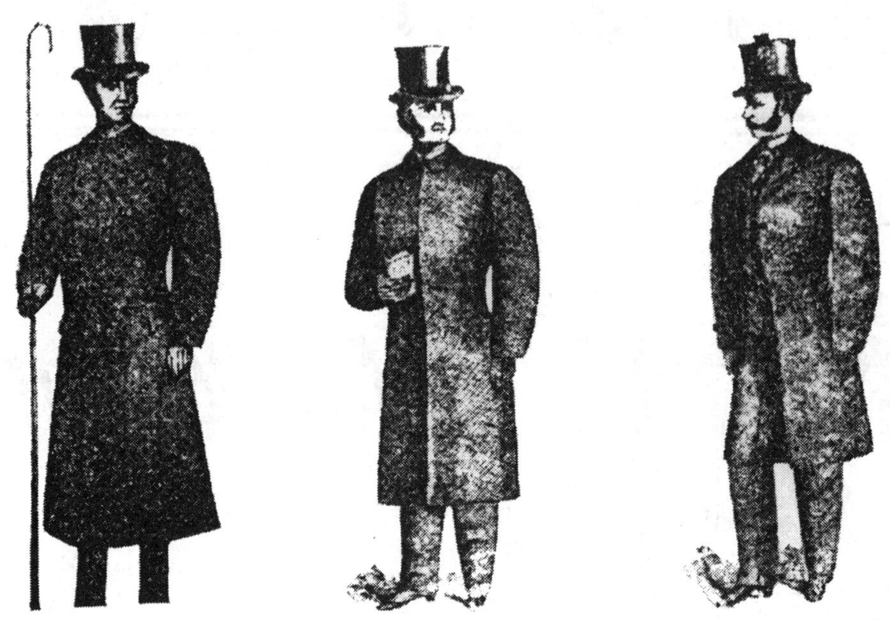

Figure 31. Professional Dress, Left, Coachman; Center, Undertaker; Right, Undertaker's Liveried Assistant

FRAMERS & LABORERS
Residential. Must have trans and the will to work. Drug test req'd. Pay depends on exp. Contact Larry at 620-9565 after 6pm.

FRAMERS. Must have tools & transp. 515-3700 or 503-397-4268

FRAMERS needed. 1-3 years experience. 625-6025

FRAMERS needed for Gresham/ Troutdale area. 663-6099

FRAMERS need sub-contractors for piece wrk & laborers 642-3446

FUNERAL. Applications being accepted for Removal Technician. Positions avail. 255-4922 Mon-Fri

FUNERAL HOME ATTENDANTS
Requires answering of funeral home door & telephone during weekend & evening hours in exchange for apartment & utils.
Send resume to:
PO Box 275, Mt Angel, OR 97362

The Loewen Group
(Company)

POSITION DESCRIPTION

Position Title: Removal Technician   **Dept.:** Removal Service

Reporting to: Manager of Removal Division

Indirect responsibility to: Regional Manager

Position Objectives: *(purpose and goals)*

To provide removal and transportation of the deceased person from the place of death to area funeral homes.

Primary duties and responsibilities: *(essential to this position)*

1. Respond to the first call for the physical removal of the deceased from the place of death. This involved working and coordinating with the Medical Examiner, Hospice and various other medical personnel as may be necessary.

2. Use a motor vehicle to go to place of death and transport deceased to funeral home. Place remains on preperation table and in cooler at funeral home.

3. Ensure that all bodies are handled with the highest standards of dignity and respect and all bodies are properly taged with identification.
   a. Use proper protective equipment at all times.
   b.
   c.
   d.
   e.
   f.
   g.
   h.
   i.

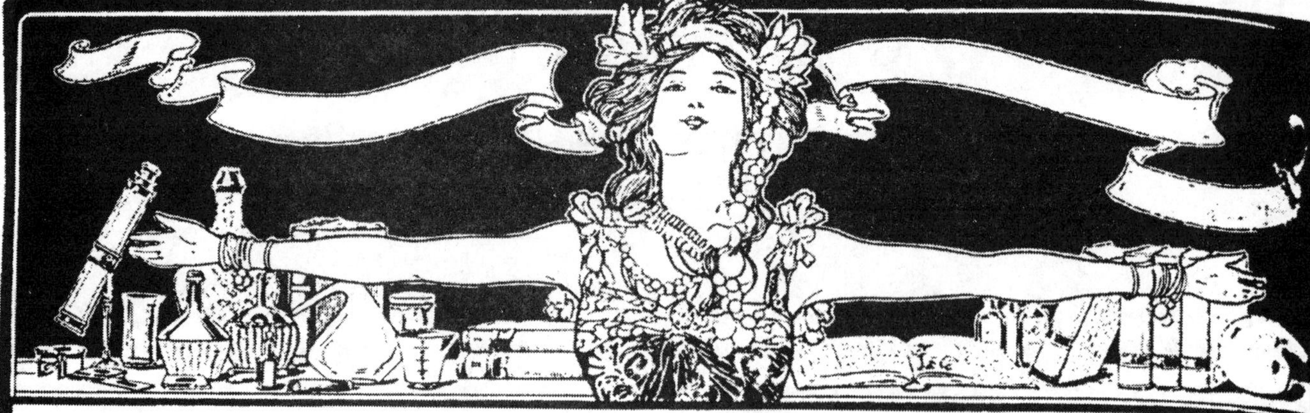

When Your Fluid Fails
Who Pays the Damage?

The forfeit of the price of one or two gallons of fluid will not atone for the damage. You pay for the failure by loss of prestige and loss of business. Isn't that so?

The safest and cheapest way is to use a fluid that can't fail—a fluid that has the

═══ STRENGTH ═══

to successfully overcome every condition that can be found in a dead body.

It is the strong fluid that carries few worries—it is the strong fluid that thoroughly preserves when the case is a difficult one, when ammoniacal gases exist and in hot, sultry weather—it is the strong fluid that establishes the embalmer's reputation for good work—and the fluids which have shown conspicuous strength in successfully preserving every kind of a case, no matter how difficult or what the conditions, and have demonstrated that they are entitled to the name "Strong Fluids" are

THE NON - POISONOUS BIG FOUR

ESCO-RADIUM, N. P., ESCO, N. P., UPTIMUM AND BESTCON, (Best Concentrated Fuid.)

It needs something more than the ordinary formaldehyde fluid to successfully overcome ammoniacal gases and hold Dropsy, Typhoid Fever cases, and stop purging in hot, sultry weather. But there is no case so difficult, no condition so bad that these fluids will not overcome every time.

They will preserve indefinitely, not only for three days, but for three years if you want it; they preserve the life-like appearance, not a putty colored, or shriveled up mummy. They are successful every time because they contain the right kind of chemicals for overcoming every kind of condition that the embalmer meets.

25 years manufacturing nothing else but embalming fluids and embalmers' supplies, a life-time of study of what is needed for the proper preservation of a body, are what have made these fluids what they are—safe and sure fluids in every instance.

Every undertaker, every embalmer, every manager, who wants positive results in all cases should send for a supply of these never-failing hot weather fluids for hot weather work and important cases.

ATTRACTIVE PARLORS

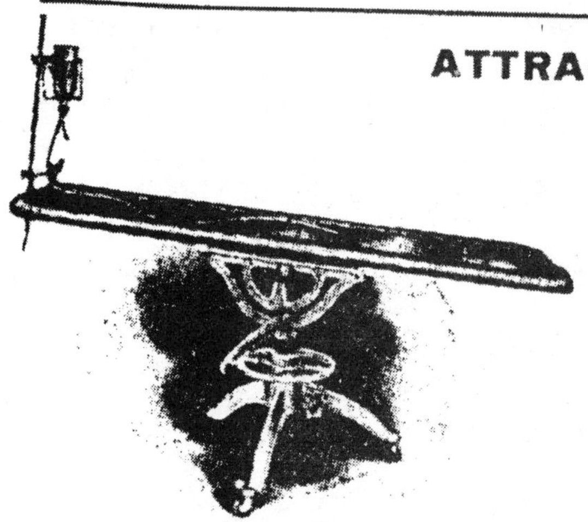

impress the public and bring business.

Nothing so adds to the attractiveness of an undertaker's establishment as an ESCO BRASS RIM MORGUE TABLE. Nothing has ever awakened so much interest in the profession as this extremely attractive business-bringer. Hundreds of shrewd, far-seeing business men have equipped their places with these tables, because they realized that they were business-bringers and are exceedingly good advertisements to their place.

THE EMBALMERS' SUPPLY CO.

WESTPORT, CONN.

CHICAGO, and LOS ANGELES, CAL.

Originators of Formaldhyde and Concentrated Embalming Fluids and Manufacturers of the Celebrated Non-Corrosive Esco Instruments, Sundries, Disinfectants and Disinfecting Appliances.

SUBTLETIES CONSTITUTE A REMOVAL
SLIGHT STAINS
QUICK SHEETING
SUMMER HAS CHANGED REMOVALS.
THEY ARE STAGNENT AND HOT,
I STRUGGLE AND SWEAT.

THE INFORMATION COMES FROM DIFFERENT
NURSES AND OLD MEN—
THE SAME DRY MOUTH AND UNCERTAINTY

THE SAME REST HOME
THE SAME TRAPPED URINE SMELL
SURROUNDED BY LUKE WARM BEDDING

THE SAME RATTLE OF CURTAIN AGAINST ROD
TIP TOEING DRESS SHOES
AS I HIDE MY TASK FROM THE SURVIVING
ROOMATE
THE HEAT MAKES IT HARD TO HIDE COLD
LOOKS, UNEMOTIONAL LABOR OF
BODY ON BED
TO BODY ON COT
PLASTIC WRAPS THE BODY WHILE LATEX
WRAPS MY HANDS,
SLIGHTLY PULLING HAIR
SLIPPING AGAINST HEAT AND SWEAT.

Last week Barry stopped by while Alex and I were working. He'd been putting in some time over at OFS (Oregon Funeral Service), and he'd been working with this real asshole. The guy had been treating Barry like a kid and Barry's been doing removals on and off for a total of almost four years. When he goes on a home removal Barry doesn't always wear gloves. Barry likes to add that personal touch to his removals, so unless fluids are present he handles the body with his bare hands. Apparently this guy didn't think wearing gloves was a personal choice, and that was just the beginning of things.

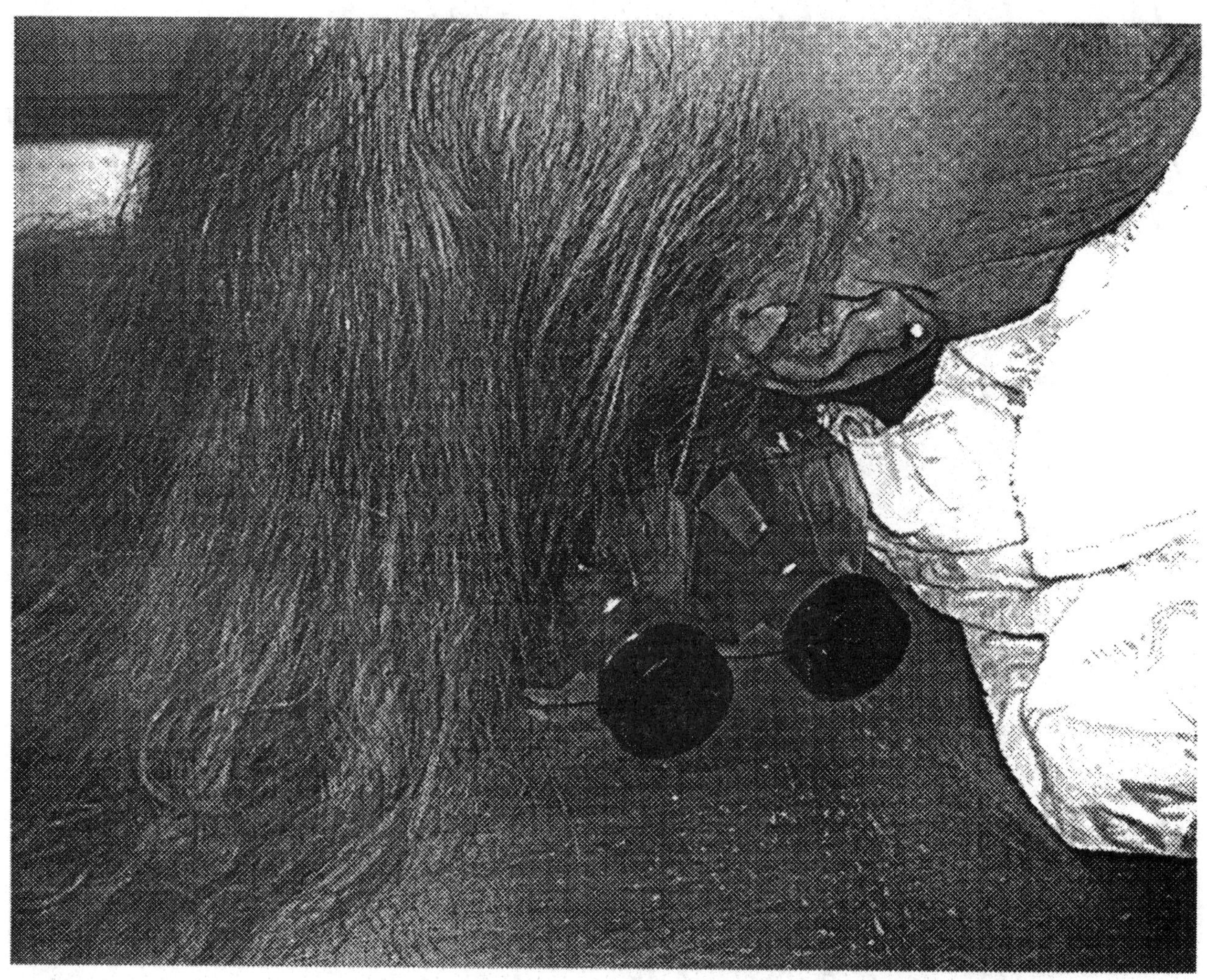

        Basically the guy wanted to do everything by the book, and Barry's just not that kind of removal technician. Barry told the guy he was a prick, and came over see me and Alex. We talked for awhile and then Barry and I went across the street to shoot some hoops. We played a game of twenty-one. I was ahead 19 to 11, but Barry came back to win. It must have been eighty or ninety degrees out and we were both wearing suits. Barry's a decent player but he fouls alot.
I worked with Barry yesterday, and even though he had a fresh cut on his hand he didn't wear gloves, but I didn't say anything about it.

Embalming Today

1. Removal and inspection of all clothing, jewelry and personal property to be given to designated employees with itemized list of such material if it has any value.

2. Removal of all bandages, surgical dressings, drains, casts, etc. Fresh surgical incisions should be opened and drained; "Dryene" or other cauterizing, disinfecting and preserving agent should be applied directly upon all wounds, incisions, bed sores, ulcers, CANCERS or any place where the skin surface is broken. It is important that this be done immediately—before arterial injection is begun.

3. Thorough disinfection, deodorization and preservation of the *entire outer surfaces* of the body by means of "De-Ce-Co Disinfecting Spray" or similar agent. Special attention should be given to mouth, nostrils, eyes, ears and hands. In cleaning and disinfecting the mouth, all dentures should be removed and cleansed before applying the "Disinfecting Spray."

4. Give special attention to the disinfection and deodorizing of the groins, plugging the rectum with cotton and also, in females, the vagina. Remove any existing ligature from the penis, on males, to allow free circulation of the embalming solution to such areas. Elevate the scrotum on all males to drain blood and/or dropsical fluid so as to permit an unobstructed circulation of the embalming solution into it.

5. Thoroughly wash all bodies with a cleansing agent, paying especial attention to hands, nails and hair. Make certain that the scalp is clean and free from vermin.

6. Relieve any existing rigor mortis, especially in the face, neck and hands.

7. Shave when necessary and when completed, dry the face and hands and apply "White Kalon Cream."

8. Pose the features and body. It is important that some thought be given to proper expression development. A few extra minutes spent in so doing may mean the difference between a satisfied or a dissatisfied family. When the body has a short, heavy neck or whenever the neck appears full, use the "Blickens Body Positioner" to relieve such fullness.

9. Make Pre-Embalming Diagnosis to enable you to classify properly each body as to Type so that specific treatment can be given to produce best possible results. Prepare solution for that Type and proceed with Embalming routine. Use caution against making incisions larger than is necessary.

10. Give consideration to the speed of injection in each individual case. Remember that senile, broken-down tissue cannot assimilate the solution as rapidly as will firmer, healthier tissue. Too rapid an injection into such flabby tissue will force the solution to the surface, producing swellings. When using an arterial chemical containing a staining dye, a spotting of color will occur if the body is injected faster than its rate of assimilation.

11. Gently massage the body during arterial injection. Cheesecloth and warm soapy water are provided for this purpose. It will materially aid in blood removal and an even tissue preservation.

The first time I really talked to Erin Fortin, he said that when his wife came out from Montana he was going to "grudge fuck" her. The phrase "grudge fuck" was followed by a hip thrust and a noise that sort of sounded like an empty mustard bottle being squeezed. A couple weeks later I learned that Erin had been fired for sexually harrassing Sandra. Alex and I obtained these notes/poems from Erin's personel file. After this whole sexual harrassment incident the Loewen Company held a mandatory sexual harrasment training session for every employee in the greater Portland area, sexual harrassment policies were posted around the office, and we were asked to sign some sort of form that would prevent us from ever filing any sort of harrassment related lawsuit against the company.

```
Barry is a pud-fucker!!   :-)          hello asshole...

     Fuck you,  asshole...    or  as Arnold
  would  say:  "Fuck you, asshole" (Terminator).
          Barry  is  a  prick-head...

    P.S.  Barry is still a  pud-fucker...

   Barry  just  wants to get down Sandra's pants
 But  then again,  who  doesn't?  XXXXXX
           Personally, I want down her shirt
         first, then work my way  down!!
                              :-P


                         :-)

    !@#$%¢&*()  +¼:"?.,
       1234567890-=½';/.,


       etc., etc., etc....

  Gotta go, time to masterbate and think
  about how Sandra will never let me sleep
  with her...  :-(
```

"SANDY"
Even as the wind blows upon
a "Sandy" Northwestern
Pacific shore...
Remember this:
There is not a man in this
whole world that desires you
More... Than I.

10 JUNE 97

To my Sandra

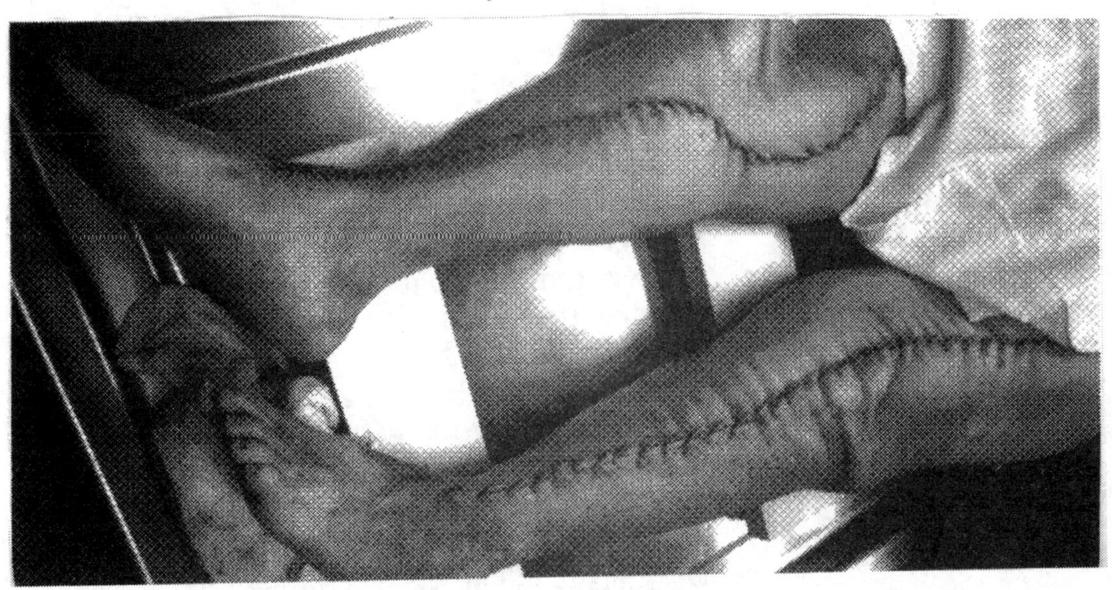

JOE SNELL REALLY LIKES SANDRA A LOT. WHO CAN BLAME HIM. SHE DRIVES EVERYONE CRAZY. SHE DROVE ERIN OVER THE EDGE. I THINK ITS HER EYES. JOE BUYS SANDRA FOOD TO SHOW HER HOW MUCH HE CARES. THE THING IS SANDRA THINKS FAT PEOPLE ARE DISGUSTING. WHEN HER AND DAN WERE GOING ON REMOVALS SHE WOULD POINT OUT FAT PEOPLE, "HOW DID THEY LET THEMSELVES GET LIKE THAT?" JOE TOOK SANDRA OUT TO TONY ROMA'S THE OTHER NIGHT AND BOUGHT HER RIBS. HE SPENT 30 BUCKS ON THEIR DINNER. TODAY WHEN DAN AND I RELIEVED SANDRA AND JOE OF THEIR SHIFT THERE WAS A NEARLY FULL BOX OF DUNKIN' DONUTS THERE. JOE HAD BOUGHT THE DONUTS, WHEN HE RELIZED THAT SANDRA THOUGHT DONUTS WERE FAT PEOPLE EATING PROBLEM FOOD HE MUST OF QUIT EATING THEM. I'LL BET SANDRA DIDN'T EVEN TOUCH ONE. JOE PROBABLY FELT REALLY SHITTY ABOUT BUYING SUCH A HUGE BOX OF DONUTS. IT WAS REALLY FAR TOO MANY. I ATE FIVE TODAY AND DAN ATE THREE. THERE ARE STILL THREE LEFT.

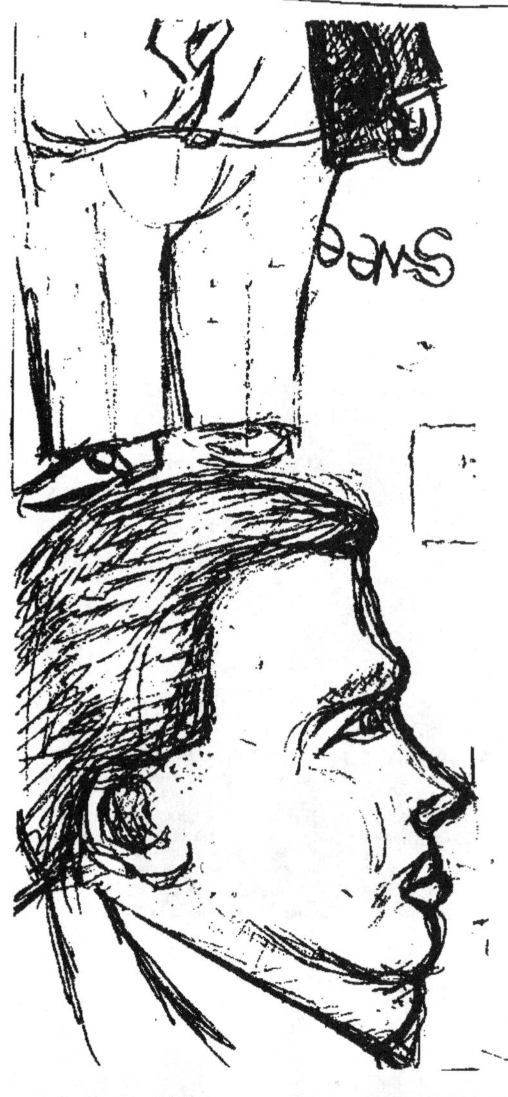

Joe Snell is moving to full time, and this means we probably won't be seeing much of him anymore. When Alex and I arrived today, Joe was just finishing up with a twenty hour shift. Joe usually leaves as soon as we both show up, but today he sort of stood around visiting. He leaned up against a cabinet, and then calmly told Alex and I that if we were still working at this job next Fourth of July, the seventh floor of the mausoleum over at PM (Portland Memorial) is a great place to check out the fireworks. Joe went on to explain that he and Sandra climbed to the top of the mausoleum after finishing a call. Joe's eyes glazed over when he was talking about it, and he even had a sort of dreamy look to him. All those fireworks reflecting off the dark windows, and Sandra standing right next to him, probably chewing gum and smelling wonderful. That Joe can appreciate something like this, and feel the need to tell us about it sort of makes me not hate him so much.

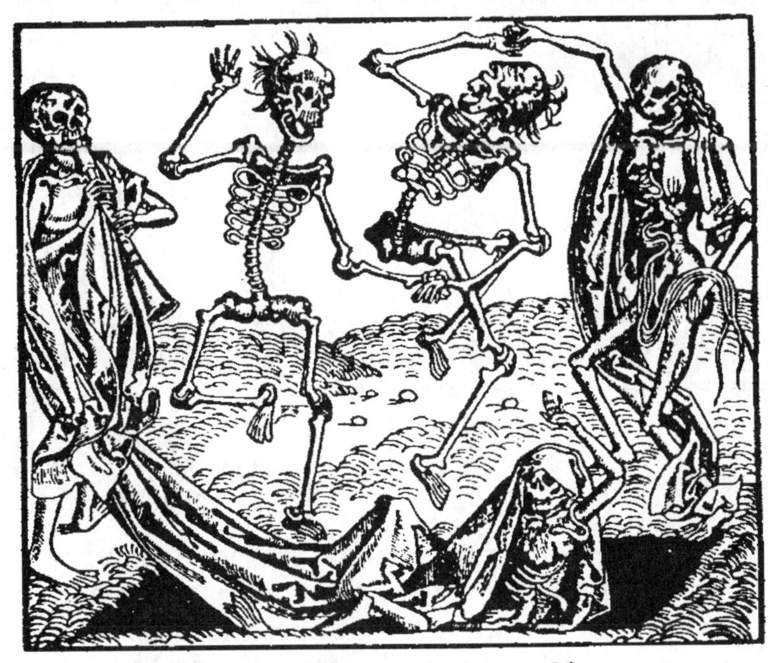

d) "Danse of Death," Nohl

Things Glenn Dixon says:

"There's nobody in the world that likes to embalm as much as me, but hey who wants to be chained to a table for eight hours a day. It's like sex, everyone likes sex, but let's face it, if you had sex eight hours a day you'd get burnt out on it.... oh, you guys might wanna take off around 1:30 for the airport, it's such a cluster fuck with all that construction going on."

"It might be gristly, but from an embalmers point of view the best way to kill your self is with carbon monoxide, you know leave the car running with the garage door closed. I don't know why, but it gives the skin a nice rosy color, and thins the blood. The blood comes right out, and the embalming fluid goes in lickity split."

"God dammit. If it's not one fuckin' thing it's another."

"It's times like this that make me wonder why I got into this fucking business. She's been in the cooler for three days, and her bloods all quagulated. I've used four fucking bottles of embalming fluid and I'm still not done."

"Actually, most people don't realize this but when women are on their period they put more blood into the sewage system, then all the funeral homes combined."

"It used to be that we'd embalm anything that came through the door, but now it's all fucking paperwork."

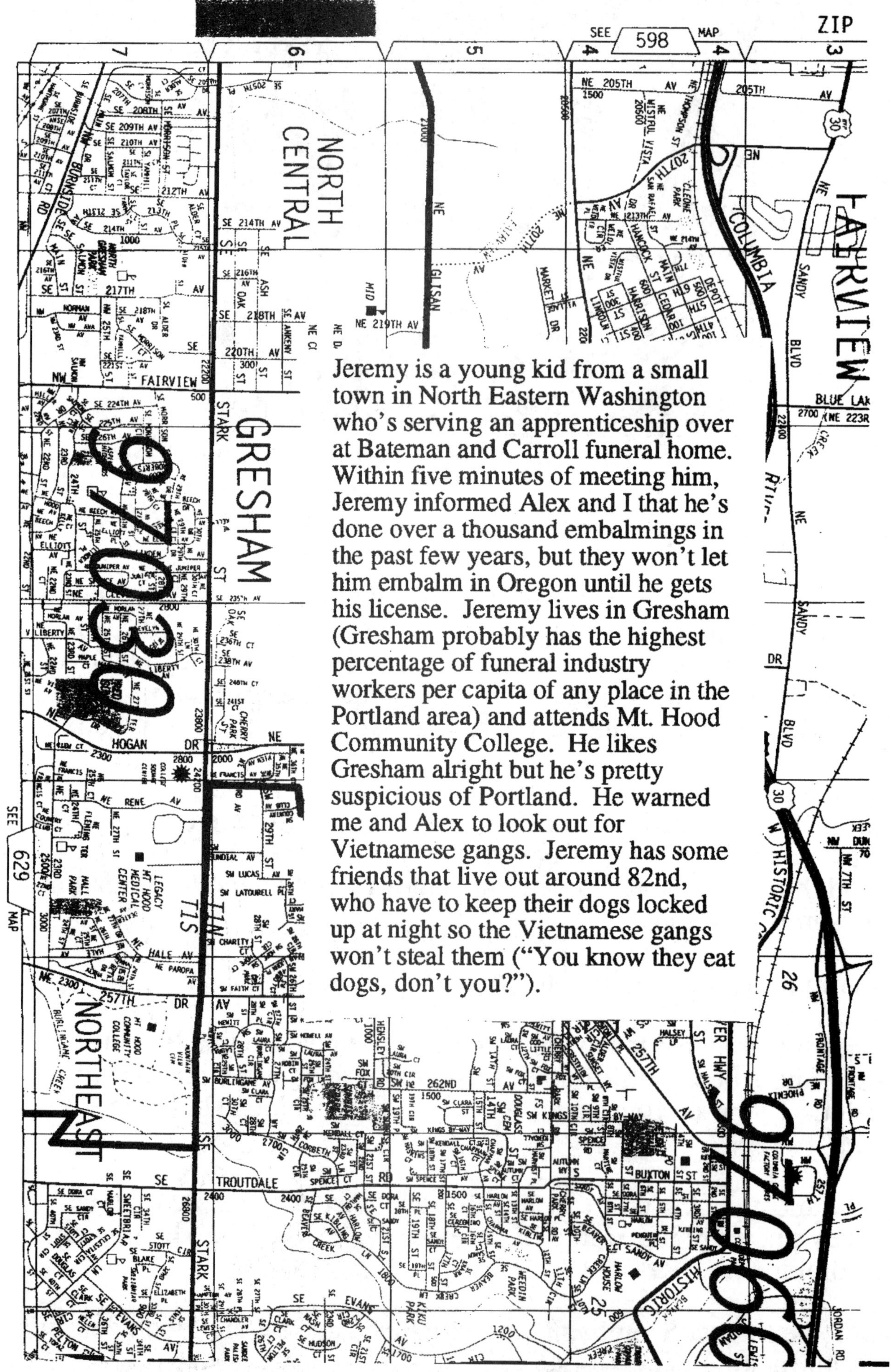

Jeremy is a young kid from a small town in North Eastern Washington who's serving an apprenticeship over at Bateman and Carroll funeral home. Within five minutes of meeting him, Jeremy informed Alex and I that he's done over a thousand embalmings in the past few years, but they won't let him embalm in Oregon until he gets his license. Jeremy lives in Gresham (Gresham probably has the highest percentage of funeral industry workers per capita of any place in the Portland area) and attends Mt. Hood Community College. He likes Gresham alright but he's pretty suspicious of Portland. He warned me and Alex to look out for Vietnamese gangs. Jeremy has some friends that live out around 82nd, who have to keep their dogs locked up at night so the Vietnamese gangs won't steal them ("You know they eat dogs, don't you?").

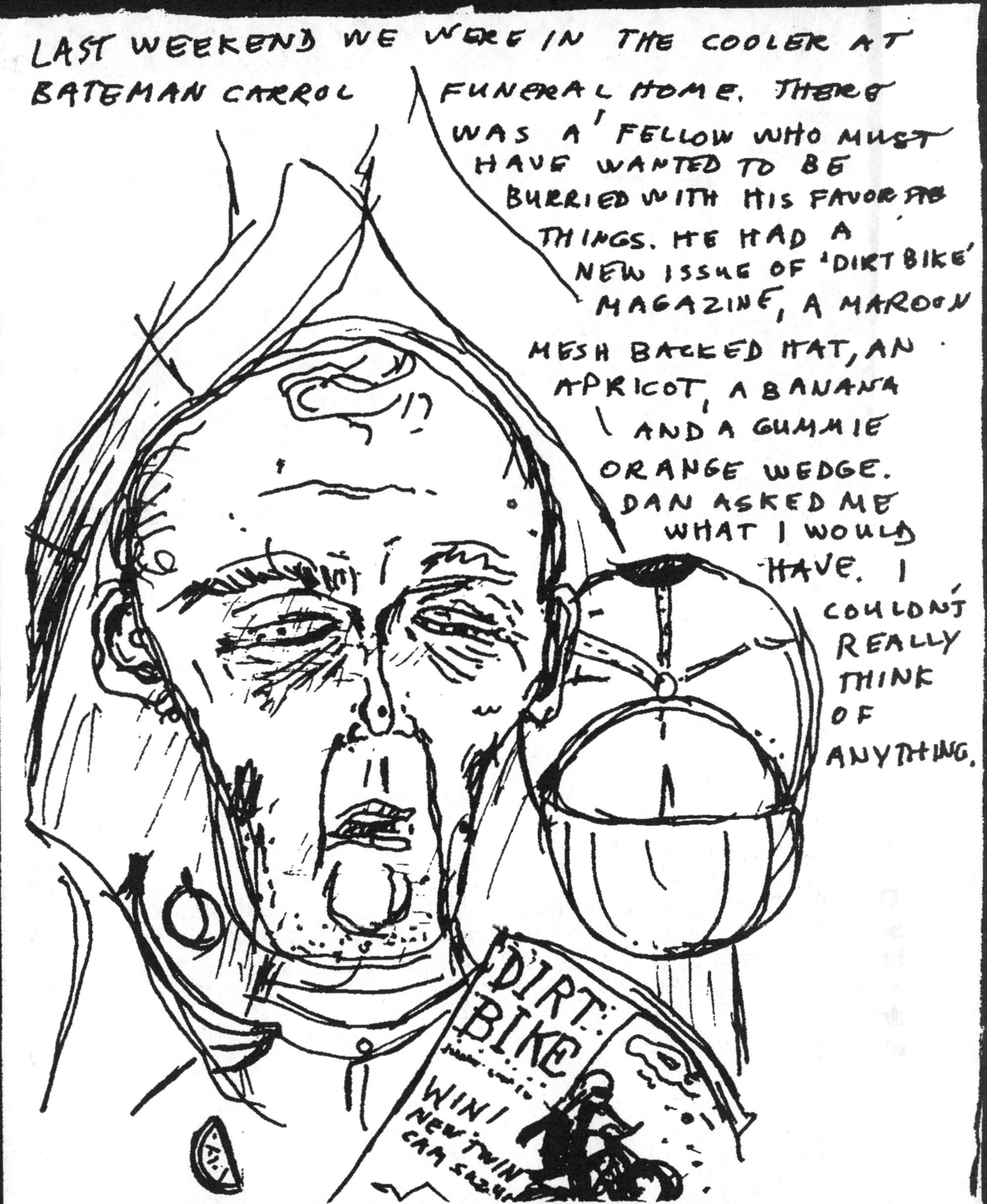

LAST WEEKEND WE WERE IN THE COOLER AT
BATEMAN CARROL   FUNERAL HOME. THERE
WAS A FELLOW WHO MUST
HAVE WANTED TO BE
BURRIED WITH HIS FAVORITE
THINGS. HE HAD A
NEW ISSUE OF 'DIRT BIKE'
MAGAZINE, A MAROON
MESH BACKED HAT, AN
APRICOT, A BANANA
AND A GUMMIE
ORANGE WEDGE.
DAN ASKED ME
WHAT I WOULD
HAVE. I
COULDN'T
REALLY
THINK
OF
ANYTHING.
DIRT BIKE
WIN!
NEW TWIN
CAM SHEW

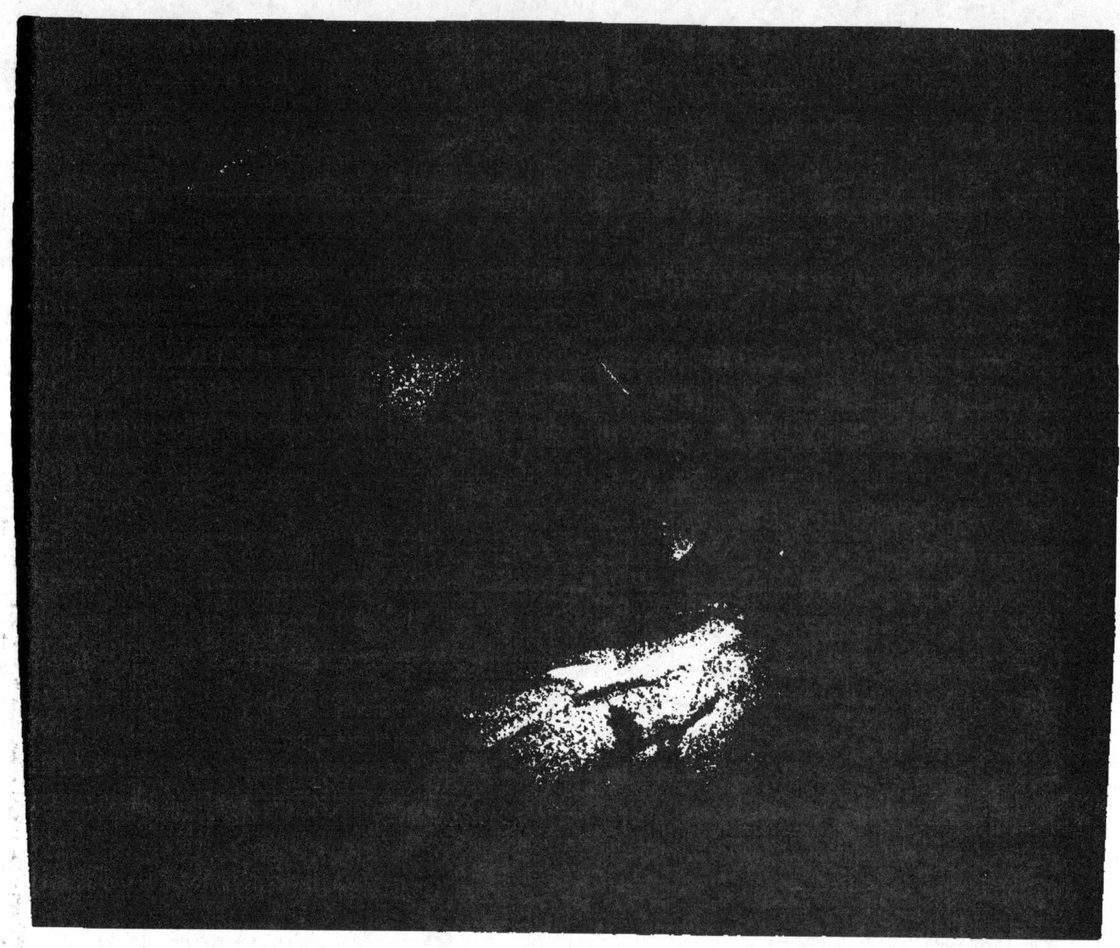

There's something about sleeping in the office that I really enjoy.
Sometimes I use a pillow from the rental caskets and lay down on the
brown and grey striped carpet. If I'm working nights I'll leave the TV on
with the sound off so it the phone rings I can see to answer it. I always
drift in and out of sleep and I generally have pointless dreams that I can't
remember.

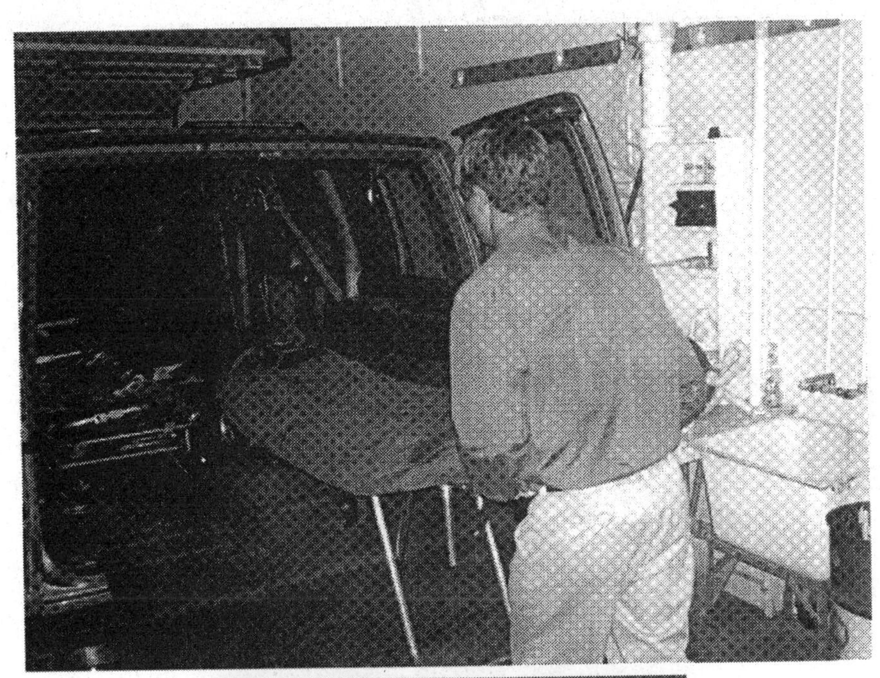

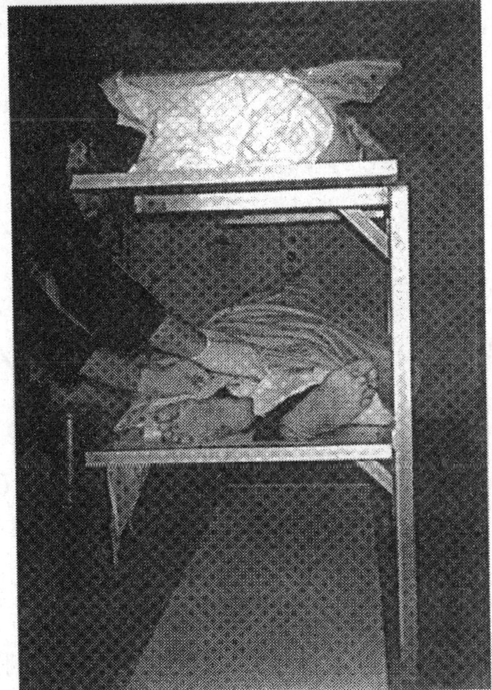

BILL LOVES NOTHING MORE THAN REMOVING JEWELRY DURING A PICK-UP. BILL EXPLAINED HIS TECHNIQUES FOR REMOVING RINGS FROM DEAD PEOPLE DURING MY INTERVIEW.

IF A RING CAN NOT BE REMOVED EASILY DUE TO RIGIMORTIS OR BLOATING SIMPLY SOAPING A FINGER MAY YIELD MORE SUCCESSFUL RESULTS.

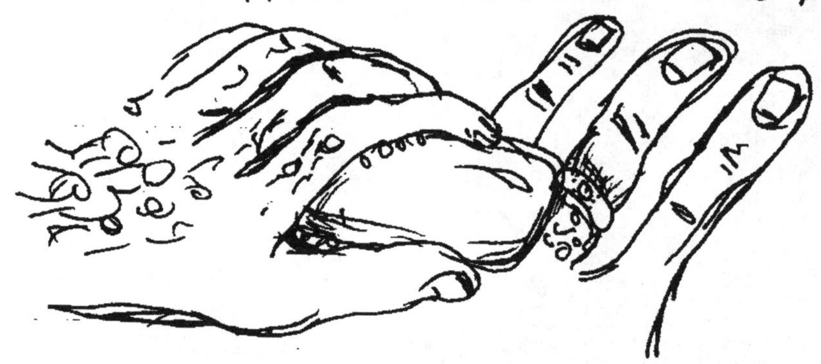

IF A RING PROVES MORE STUBBORN THAN SOAP, SOAP AND STRING USED TOGETHER WILL ALMOST CERTAINLY GET A RING OFF EVEN THE MOST BLOATED LOVED ONE. FIRST SOAP THE FINGER (SEE ABOVE) THEN SLIDE A STRING UNDER THE RING, BETWEEN RING AND FINGER. YOU SHOUD THEN BE ABLE TO JUST TWIRL THE RING OFF.

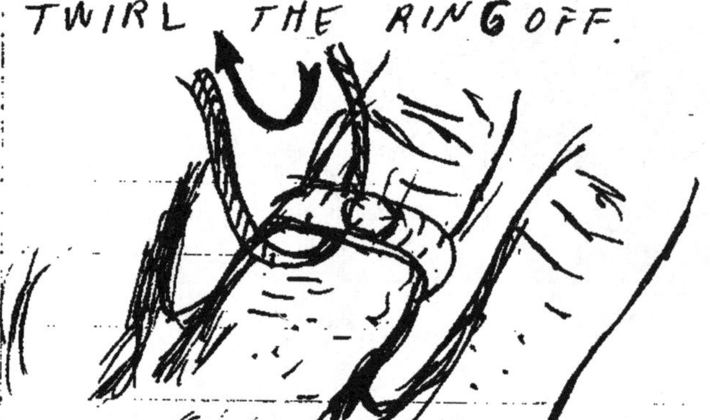

IF THE FINGER IS TOO BLOATED TO ALLOW STRING UNDER THE RING YOU MAY USE AN EMBALMING NEEDLE TO PUSH THE STRING THROUGH.

THE FIRST CALL

IN THESE modern days, no one questions what shall be done immediately following the death of a relative or friend. The embalmer is immediately called and everything is left for him to supervise.

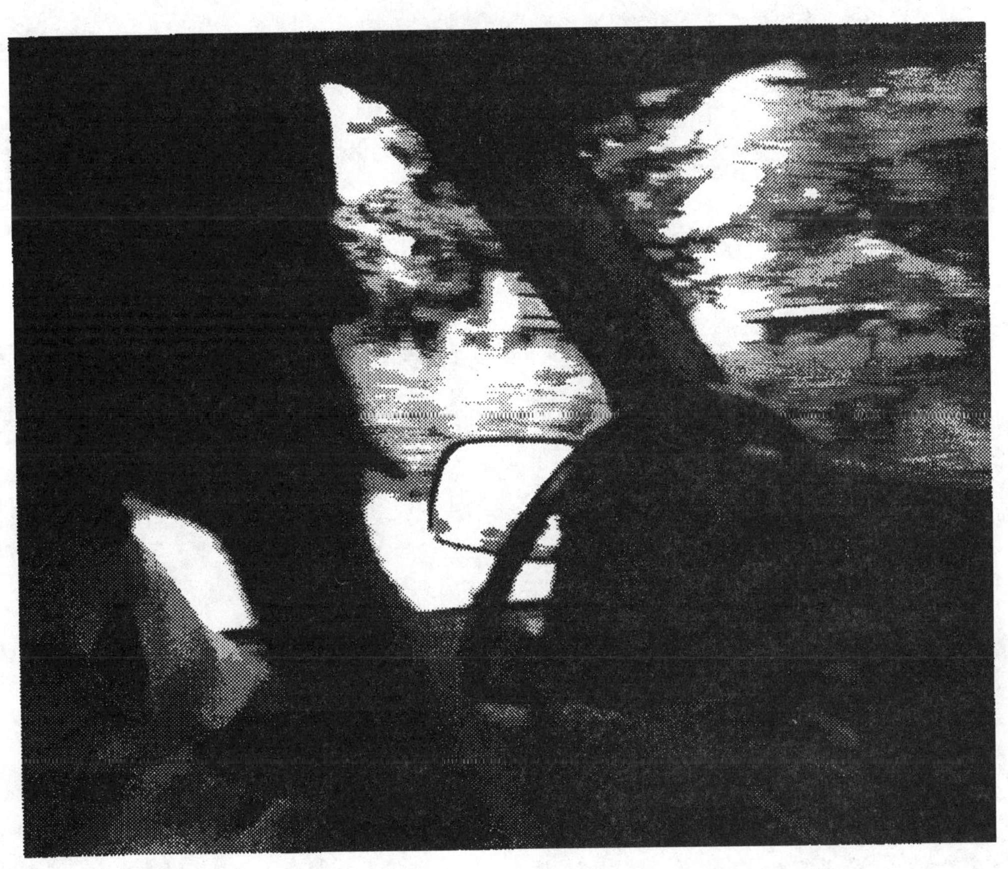

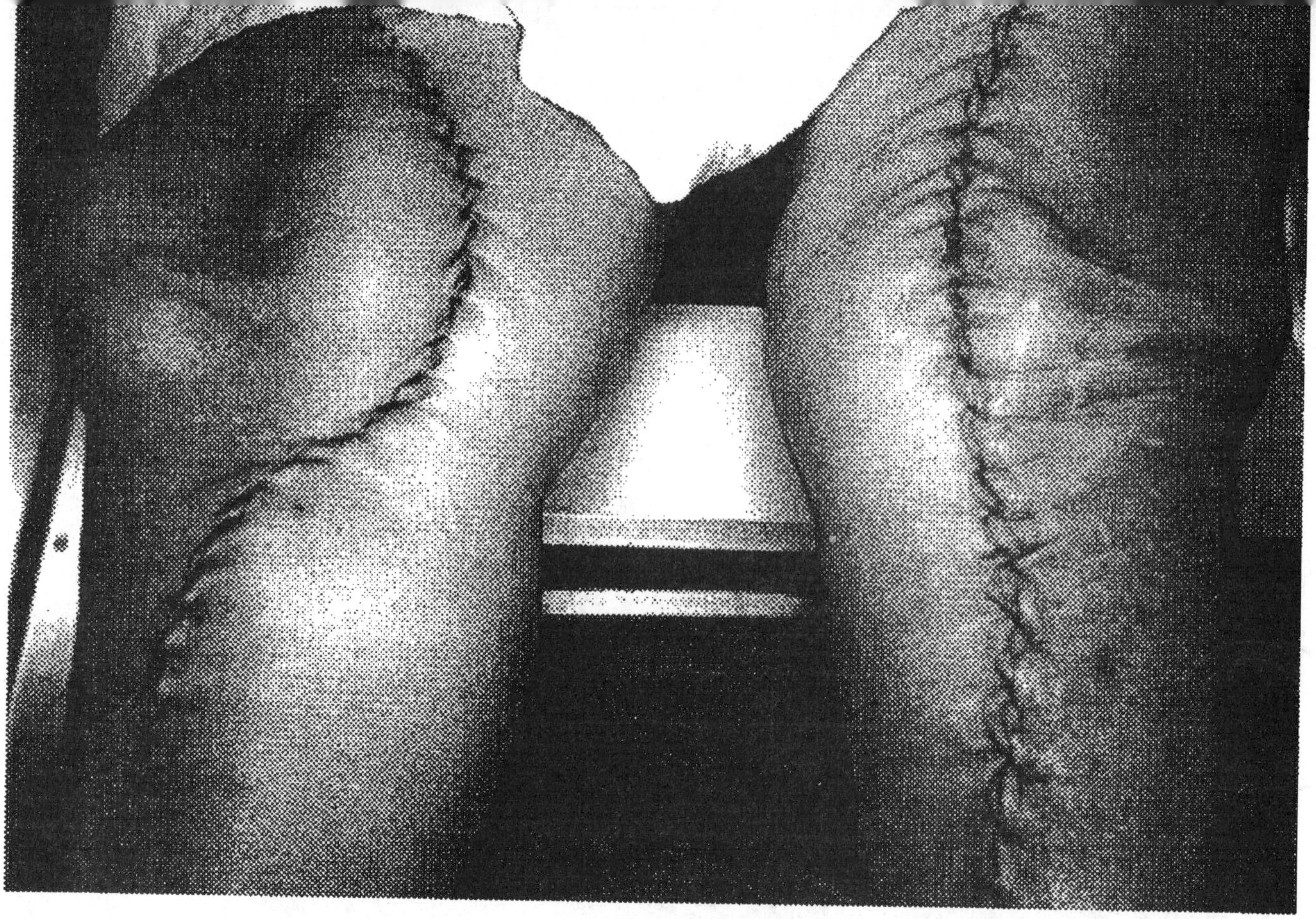

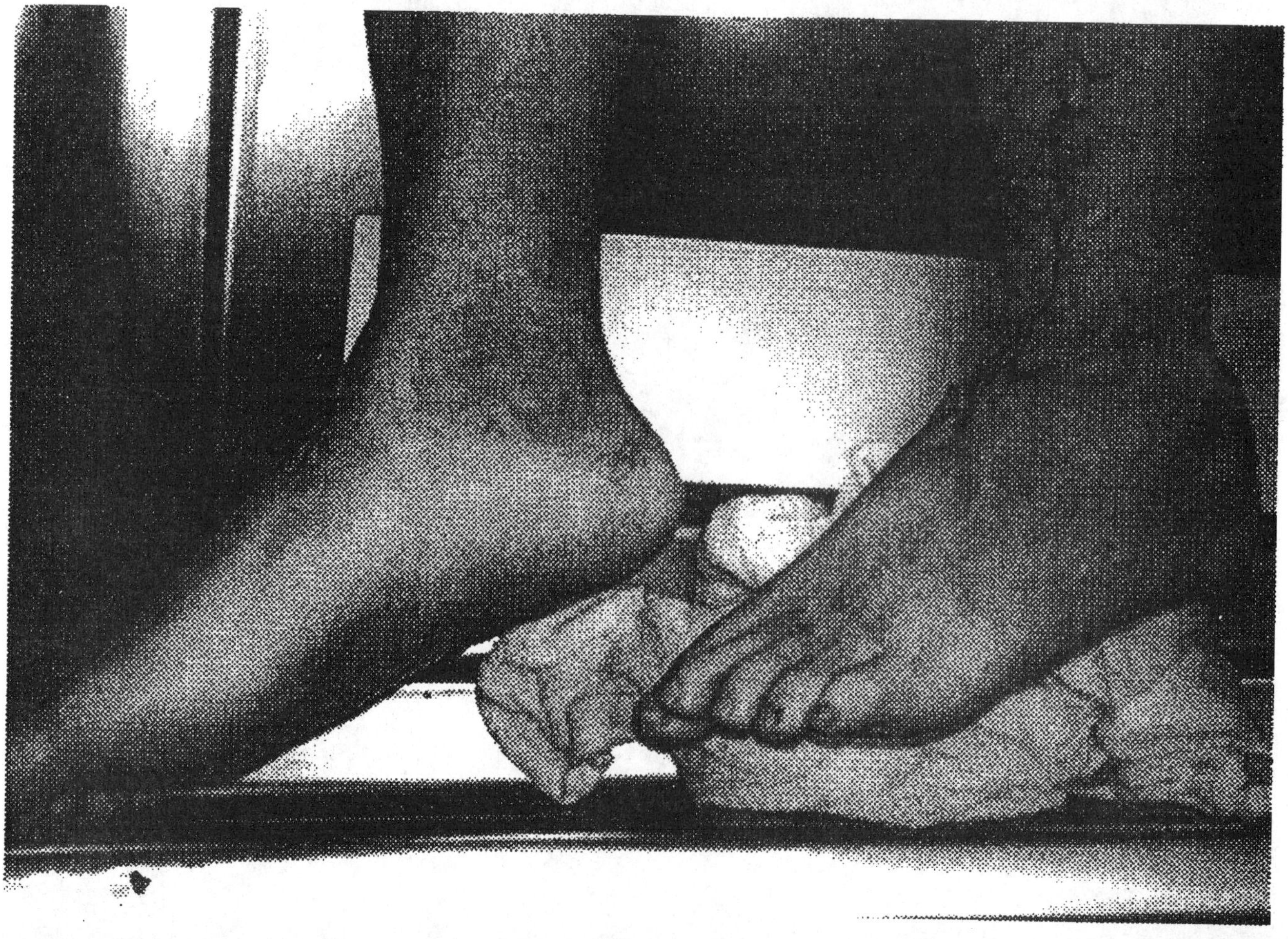

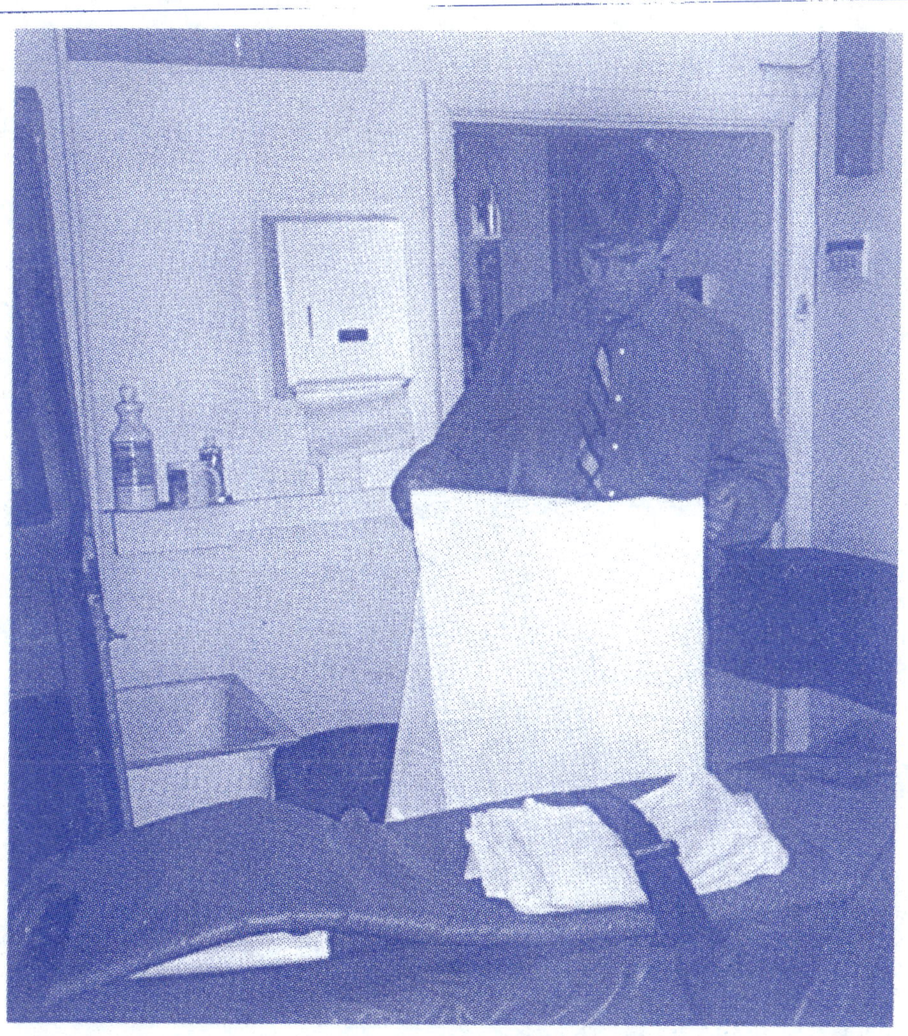

Closing the eyes is one of the most important operations. Eyes improperly or unnaturally closed speak forcibly against an embalmer's qualifications. Eyes should always be closed naturally. The lids should never be overlapped. No one closes his eyes that way in life.

Once when I was working by myself I let a body fall on the floor and this is about the biggest mistake you can make as a removal technician. He weighed atleast 250 pounds and he was icey cold through my latex gloves. I would drag him by his arm and yellow T-shirt half way onto the cot and then he would slide off again. There's no ventilation in the Peakes basement and it was one of the hotter days of the summer. I kept hitting my head on the ceiling, and I had to change gloves twice because I was sweating so much. I struggled for around twenty minutes and I wanted to kick the body but I pulled him onto a board and pushed him across the floor into the cooler.

08-09-97

Cindy/Dale,

While transferring Kenneth D from the removal cot to the hydrolic lift, his body fell to the ground I'm working alone today, and I was unable to lift Kenneth from the ground onto my cot. I placed him on a board and slid him onto the floor of the cooler. I realize that this will be an inconvenience for you, as it will be just as difficult for you to lift Kenneth from the floor as it was for me. Tommorow I will be working with a partner, and I plan to return to Peakes and place Kenneth on one of the shelves. Once again I'm sorry for the inconvenience, but at this point, this seems to be the best option

Dan
Portland Service Center

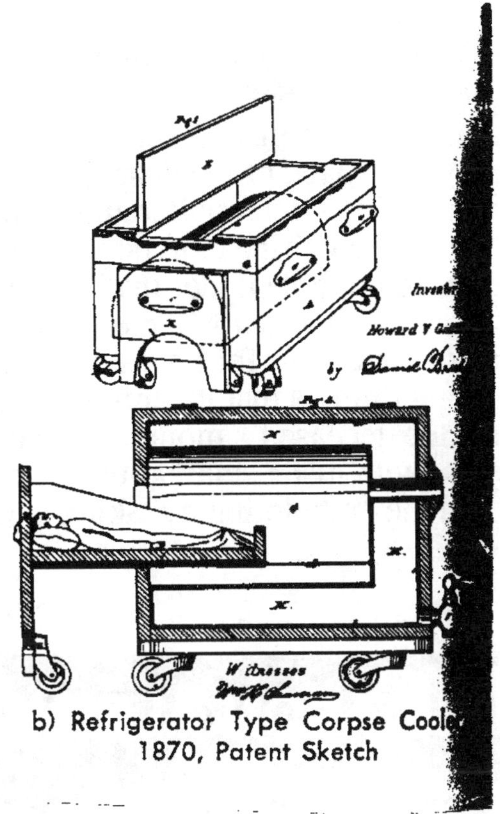

b) Refrigerator Type Corpse Cooler
1870, Patent Sketch

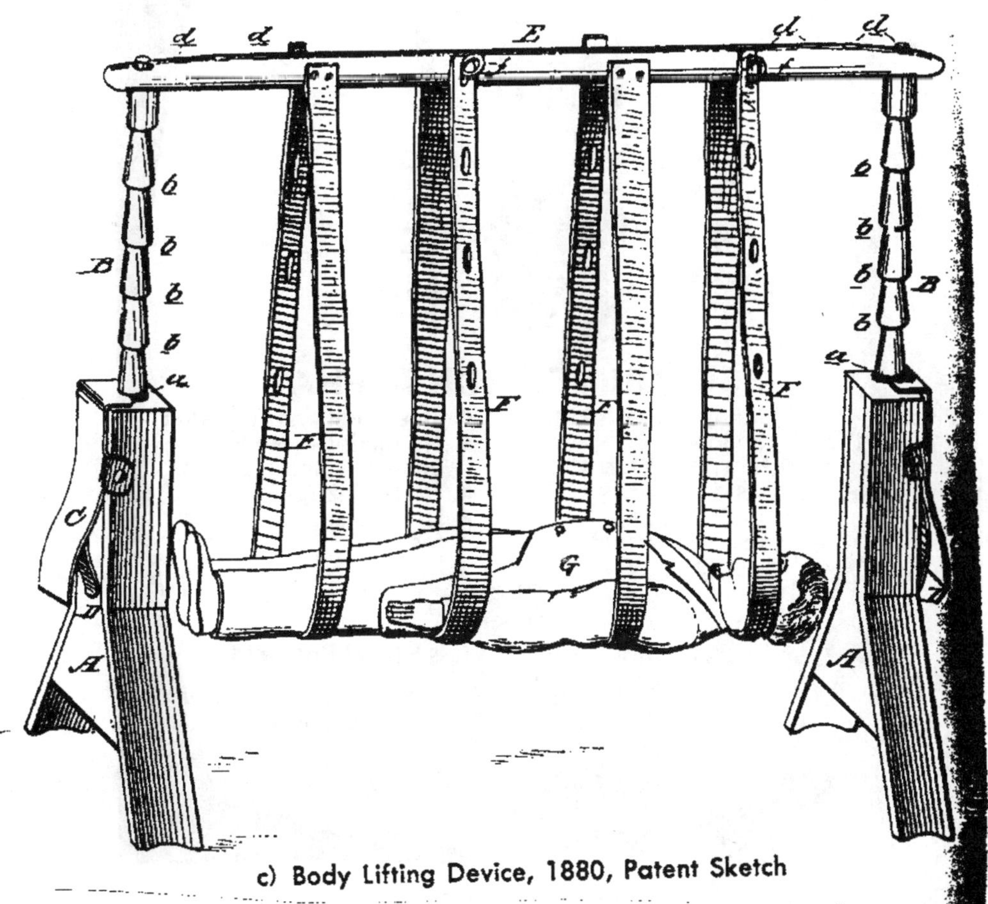

c) Body Lifting Device, 1880, Patent Sketch

Last weekend, Glenn Dixon showed us his special "through the nose" technique for setting somone's mouth before embalming. A large needle is attached to a thick fishing line type string and inserted through the nose. The needle is brought through the back of the nose into the mouth, and then out through the bottom of the chin. Glenn pulled down the lower lip so we could see how the needle passed under the chin bone. The needle is brought back up through a different hole under the the chin, making it possible for the embalmer to tie a knot that will close and set the mouth. I've never really had much of a memory for knot tying, so this may not be exactly right, but the important thing is that the through the nose method enables the embalmer to set the deceased's mouth without disturbing the lips. This method leaves you with just a small knot in the left nostril, so you can find out if Glenn did the embalming by taking a quick look up the deceased's nose.

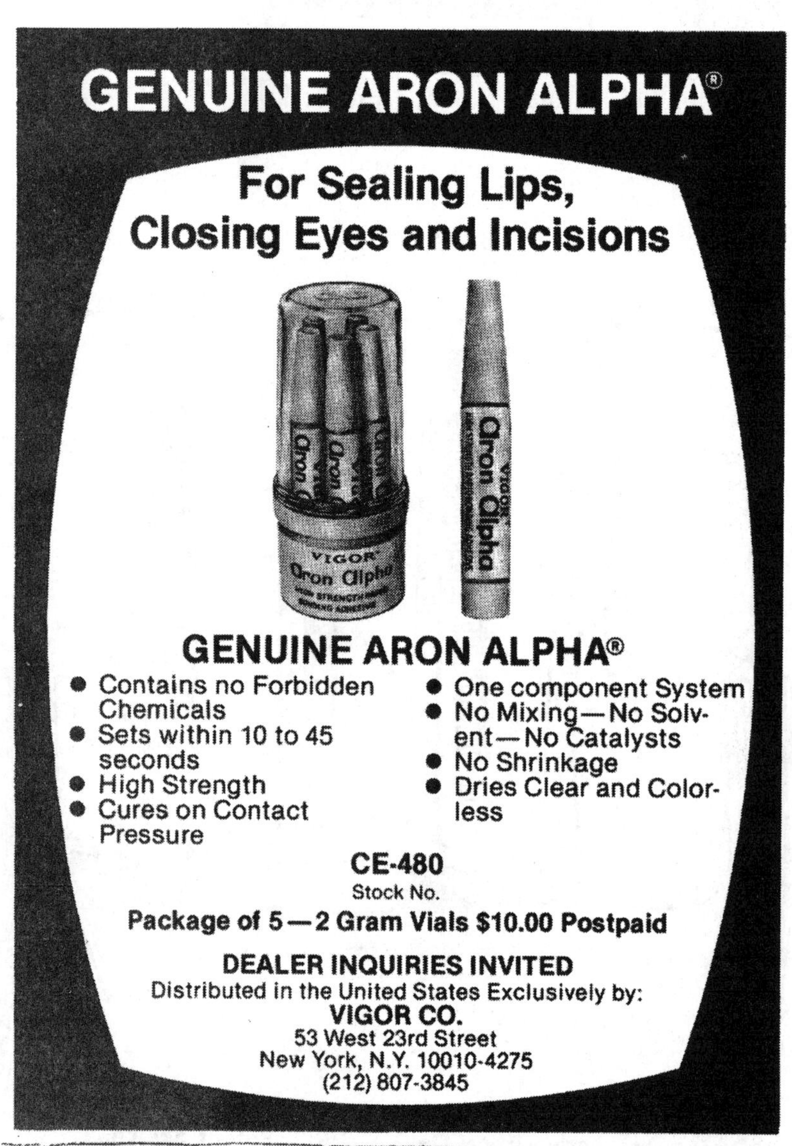

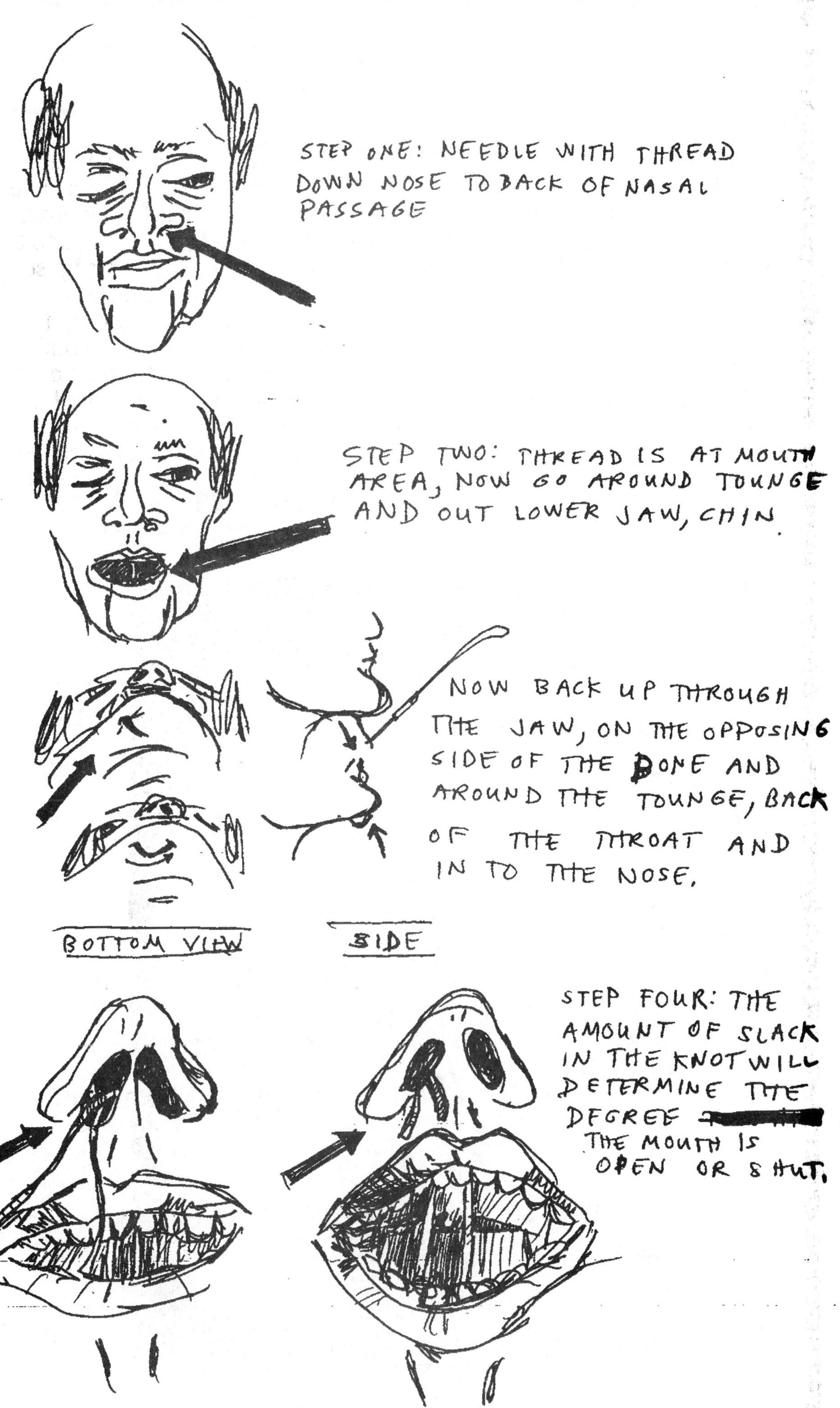

STEP ONE: NEEDLE WITH THREAD DOWN NOSE TO BACK OF NASAL PASSAGE

STEP TWO: THREAD IS AT MOUTH AREA, NOW GO AROUND TOUNGE AND OUT LOWER JAW, CHIN.

A
B

NOW BACK UP THROUGH THE JAW, ON THE OPPOSING SIDE OF THE BONE AND AROUND THE TOUNGE, BACK OF THE THROAT AND IN TO THE NOSE,

BOTTOM VIEW

SIDE

STEP FOUR: THE AMOUNT OF SLACK IN THE KNOT WILL DETERMINE THE DEGREE THE MOUTH IS OPEN OR SHUT.

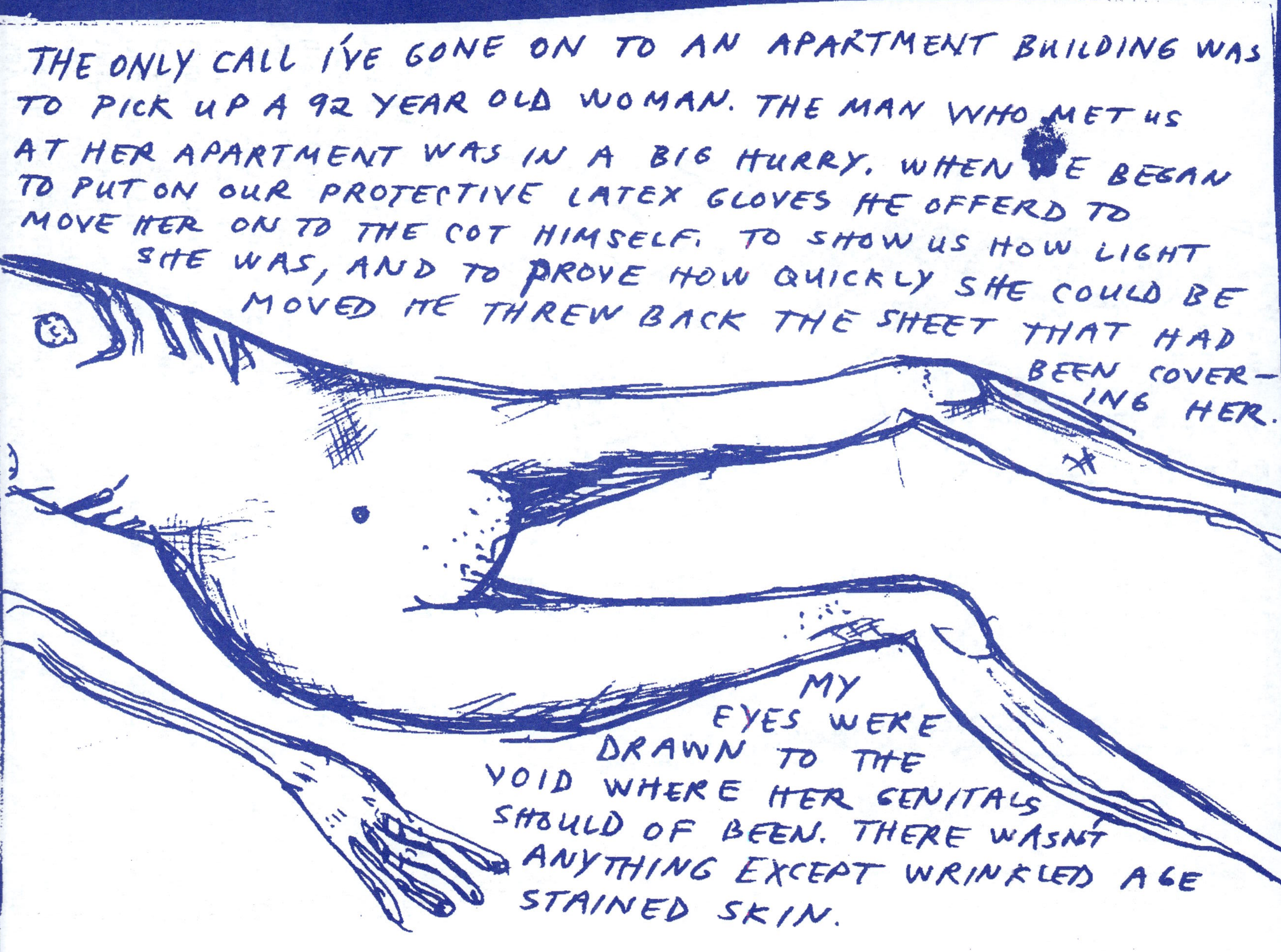

THE ONLY CALL I'VE GONE ON TO AN APARTMENT BUILDING WAS
TO PICK UP A 92 YEAR OLD WOMAN. THE MAN WHO MET US
AT HER APARTMENT WAS IN A BIG HURRY. WHEN WE BEGAN
TO PUT ON OUR PROTECTIVE LATEX GLOVES HE OFFERD TO
MOVE HER ON TO THE COT HIMSELF. TO SHOW US HOW LIGHT
SHE WAS, AND TO PROVE HOW QUICKLY SHE COULD BE
MOVED HE THREW BACK THE SHEET THAT HAD
BEEN COVER-
ING HER.
MY
EYES WERE
DRAWN TO THE
VOID WHERE HER GENITALS
SHOULD OF BEEN. THERE WASN'T
ANYTHING EXCEPT WRINKLED AGE
STAINED SKIN.

For my first three weeks as a removal technician I worked with Jason Pfau. He seems like he should be a real interesting guy but we never had much to say to each other. Jason has demonic tattoos that extend from his wrist to his elbows. He likes to roll up his sleeves when he's eating so everyone can see his tats. He has a stud in his tongue that he's constantly playing with, and he wears one of those skull rings with spikes around it. On top of all this he plays bass for The Delinquents. You would think he'd be a lot of fun to pick up bodies with but all he ever did was watch TV. Jason does this thing with his hands where he puts his fingers together and then splays them out with a quick snap. Sandra thought Jason was a crank fiend and she might be right. Once, Alex and I were hanging out with him after our shift, and his eyes did seem to be darting from side to side quite a bit, and his nose started spontaneously bleeding. About a week later Jason was fired for showing up to work drunk. (actually Bill just sent him home after Sandra ratted him out, but he never came back to work after that) I sort of miss Jason and if you ever go to a Delinquents show you should buy him a beer and ask him about his days as a removal technician.

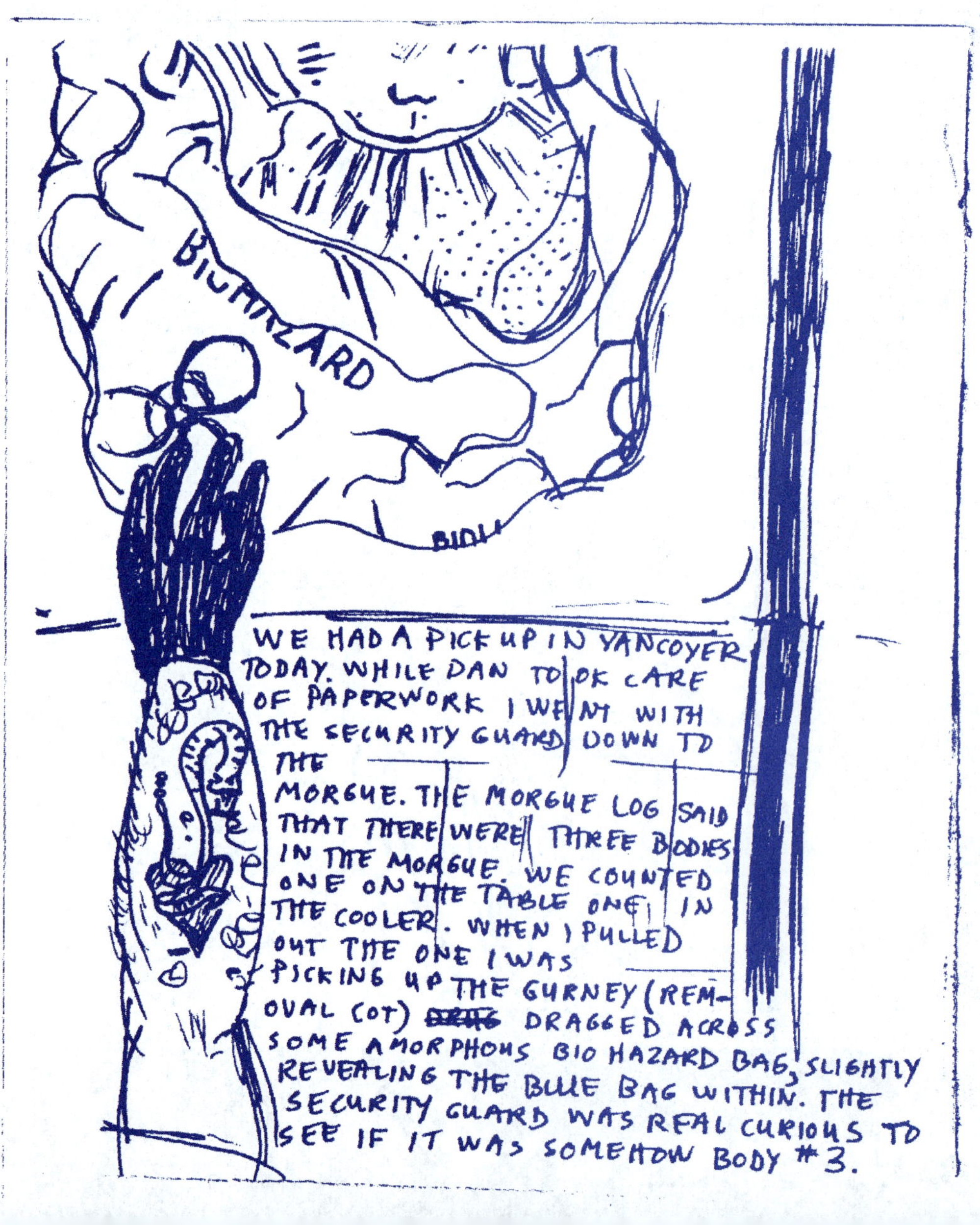

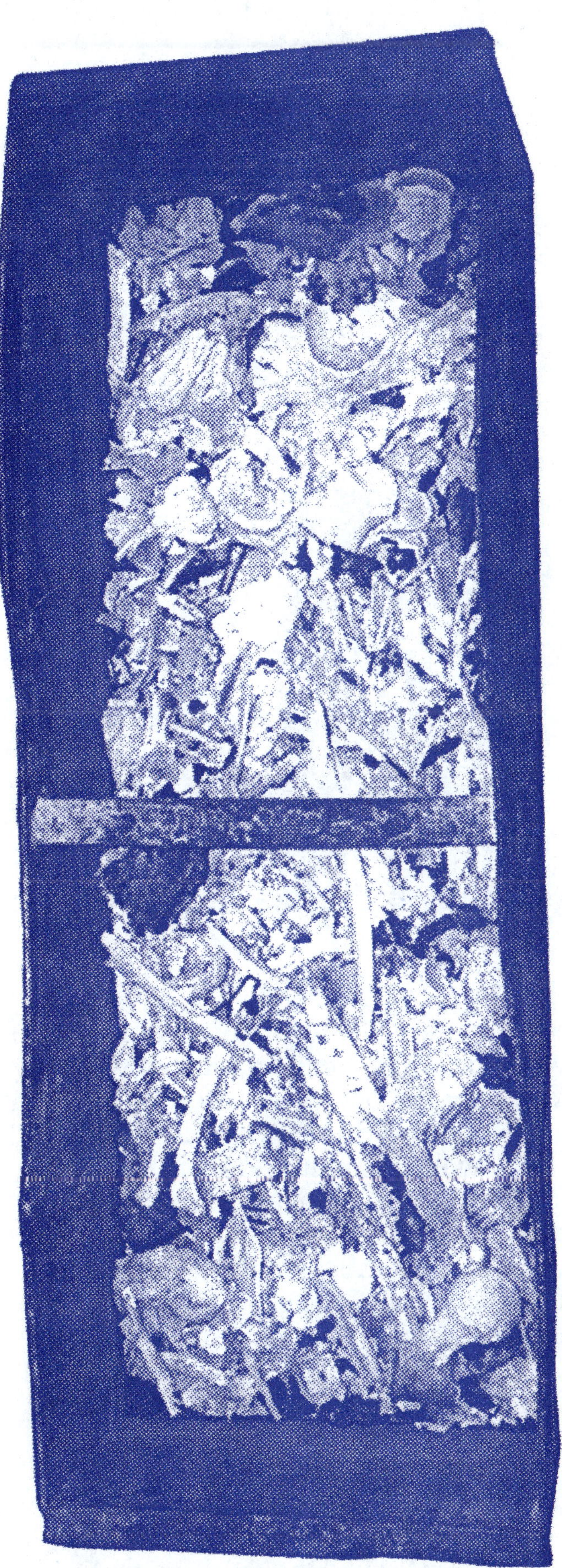

These are "Cremains" from Young's Funeral Parlor in Tigard. Most people don't realize that a cremated body leaves this many bones. The bones are crushed into a powder and then placed in an urn or some other memorial container. Jeremy from Bateman and Carrol says that the only part of his job that he doesn't like is cremating bodies. About half way through the cremation process he has to take a shovel and stir what's left of the body around, to make sure everything gets equally burnt.

After working as removal technicians for well over a month, Alex and I are becoming quite good at our job. This weekend we had three removals and they were all nearly flawless.

Removal #1
An older woman had died at Mt. Hood Medical Center and we needed to trasport her to Bateman and Carrol Funeral Home. Our sheet work on this removal was amazing (see issue #1 for a description of the sheeting process). I have to admit that it did help that the deceased was wearing pants. Normally we're worried about handling the buttocks area of the body, because we don't want to come into direct contact with any fluids. The presence of those pants allowed us to wrap the woman in a sheet and pull her from her bed onto our removal cot with a quickness and precision that even an experienced technician would admire.

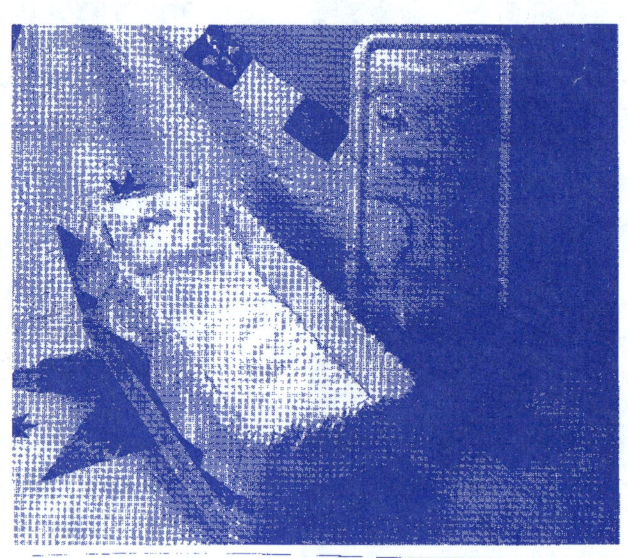

Removal #2
We were removing a woman from her home in Milwaukie, and Alex and I were a little bit nervous because we'd smoked a small amount of weed beforing coming to work. However, our confidence and skill as technicians allowed us to overcome any problems that you might expect to be caused by being a little stoned. It took us around twenty minutes to find the house, and as usual I did the talking. I find that if I speak in a calm, barely audible voice the families are easier to work with. After getting the appropriate information from the family, we brought the removal cot into the living room and placed it on the right side of the bed. The only awkward moment came when we grabbed small sized latex gloves from the cot. We had to pause to dig out larger sized gloves, but then we were able to proceed with our work. The family had wrapped the beloved in the lavender sheet that she was sleeping on, so we simply needed to slide the sheet from the bed onto our cot. Alex supported the head while the family and I moved the body. We paused to let the daughter climb onto the body and kiss her face, before zipping up the cot, still leaving the face exposed. After wheeling the cot outside and loading it into the van, we informed the family that the funeral director would be in touch with them tomorrow.

Removal #3
Once again an older woman had died, this time at Portland Adventist
Medical Center. First we checked into admitting and they directed us to the
appropriate floor, where we obtained the necessary paper work and signed
for the release of the body. The body was already bagged so it wasn't
necessary to use a sheet or plastic. Hospitals use thin, white, nylon bags
that are water resistant. We simply needed to unzip the bag in order to

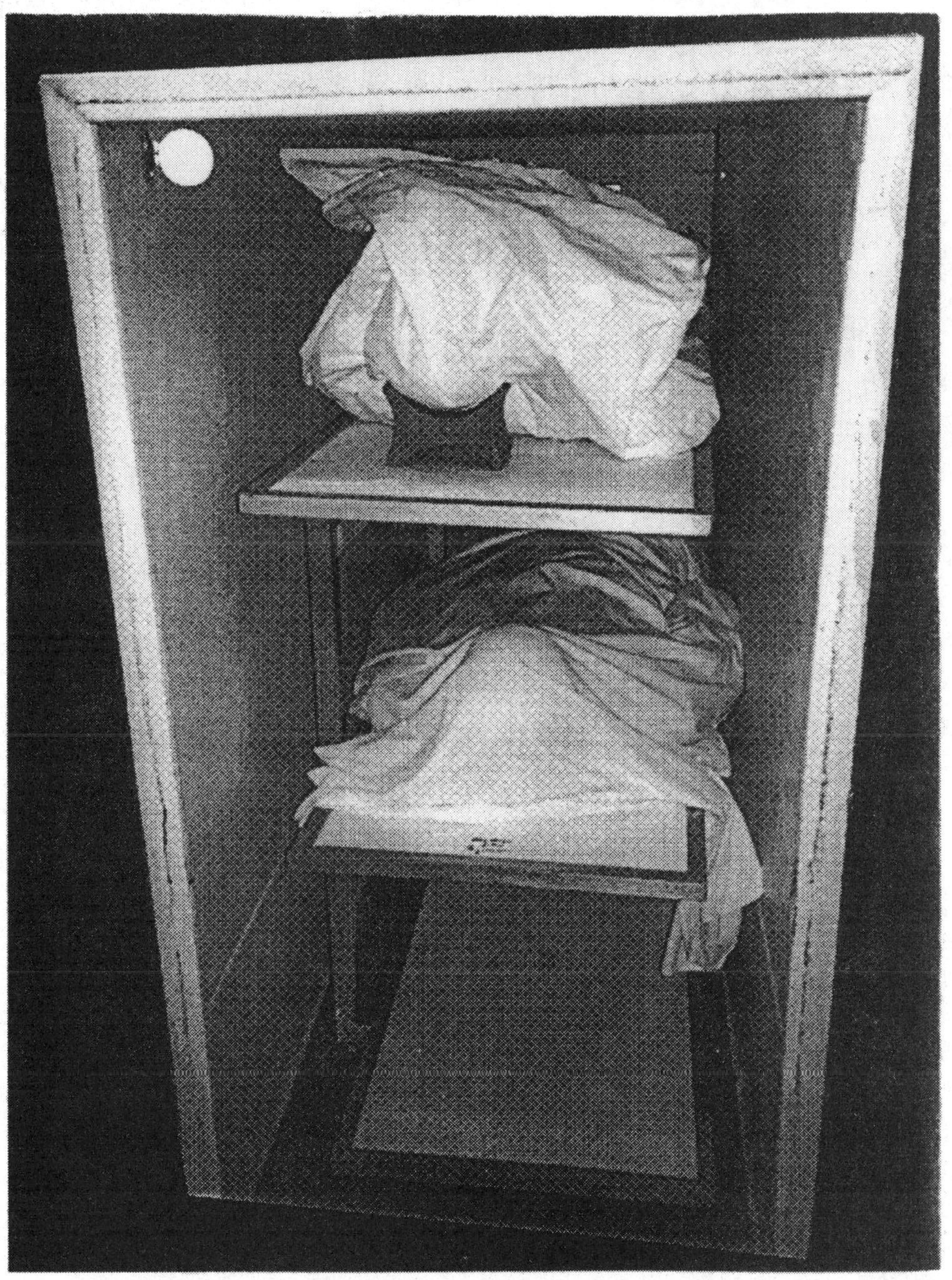

attach a Loewen identification tag to the woman's ankle. The process of
wrapping the white plastic band around the ankle and snapping it closed is
becoming extremely familiar to me. Ankles generally have a yellowish
color and the toenails look as if they haven't been trimmed recently. Once a
man's ankle was so bloated that we needed to attach two tags together in
order to reach around it.

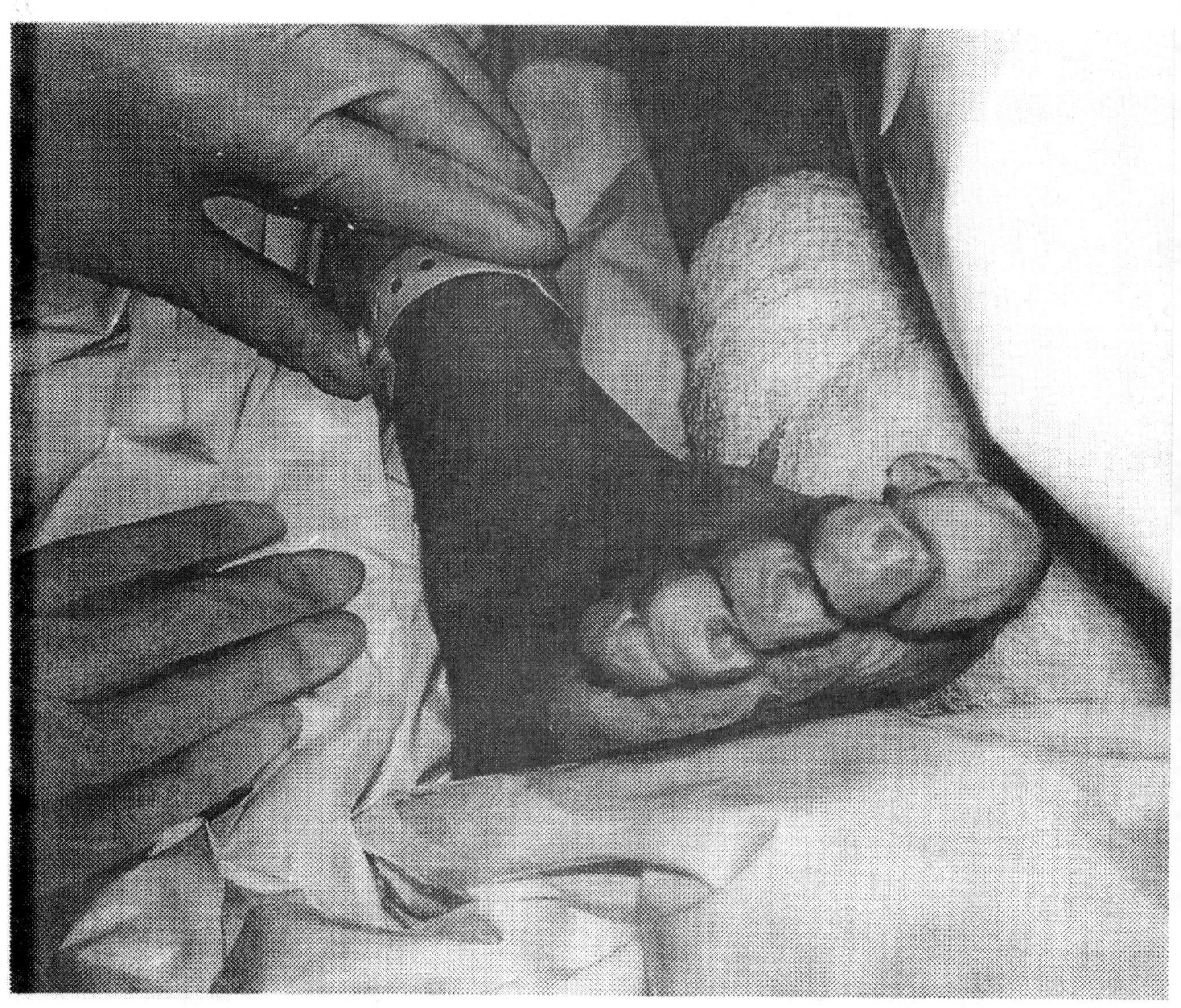

Inform us when a colleague or immediate family member dies.

Mail obituaries to The Removal Technician, 605 SW 5th, Newport, OR 97365 Please include a contact name and number so further information can be gathered, if necessary. Also, if you are notifying us about the death of an immediate family member, please state his or her relationship to the funeral director and funeral home affiliation.

Removal Technician
© 2014 Alex Hubbard, Dan Mains, and Primary Information

ISBN: 978-0-9906896-2-1

Primary Information
41 Grand Street, Ground Floor
New York, NY 10013
www.primaryinformation.org

Printed in an edition of 1,000

Special thanks to Michael Eby and Aaron Kaplan.

Primary Information is a 501(c)(3) non-profit organization that receives generous support through grants from The Andy Warhol Foundation for the Visual Arts, The National Endowment for the Arts, the Graham Foundation for Advanced Studies in the Fine Arts, the Foundation for Contemporary Arts, the New York State Council on the Arts, the Stichting Egress Foundation, and individuals worldwide.